IT'S A FUNNY GAME

'I have been lucky in that throughout my life I have spent a lot of time laughing. So much so that I have often been accused of not taking anything seriously. Not true really, but I know what people mean. I have been blessed (?) with a sense of the ridiculous and a vivid imagination, plus a mind which is automatically tuned to trying to make a pun or joke at every possible opportunity.'

True to form, Brian Johnston never misses a chance to tell a funny story or witty anecdote in this continuation of his life story which began with *It's Been a Lot of Fun*. No one can fail to enjoy what he calls 'the meanderings of a remarkably happy and lucky person, to whom life – like cricket – is a funny game and still A LOT OF FUN.'

Also by Brian Johnston in *Star*

IT'S BEEN A LOT OF FUN

IT'S A FUNNY GAME

Brian Johnston

Star

A STAR BOOK

published by
the Paperback Division of
W. H. ALLEN & Co. Ltd

A Star Book
Published in 1983
by the Paperback Division of
W.H. Allen & Co. Ltd
A Howard and Wyndham Company
44 Hill Street, London W1X 8LB

First published in Great Britain by W.H. Allen & Co. Ltd,
1978.

Printed in Great Britain by
Hunt Barnard Printing Ltd., Aylesbury, Bucks.

ISBN 0 352 31278 5

TO PAULINE

a second offering with all my love

Contents

Acknowledgements

My grateful thanks to all of the following:

Les Bailey for his streaker poem – Mrs Alan Hamilton for her late husband's poem *The Cricketer's If* – *The Times* for the reproduction of an article by Michael Leapman – an unknown lady for her parody of the Crispin Day Speech from Shakespeare's *Henry V*. And to my daughter, Clare, Linda Green and Wendy Wimbush for their skill in deciphering my writing.

Preface

I have been put into bat again – I have been asked to follow on. Any person who writes *two* autobiographies must be egotistical. But any person who refuses when graciously asked has to be pretty strong-minded. If Jim Swanton had not pinched the title first I might even have called this book *Follow On*. But I have chosen its present title because so often in the commentary box I have found myself saying: 'It is impossible to forecast what will happen. CRICKET IS A FUNNY GAME.' In fact, this is the most common of all cricket clichés – or *clish* as that great man Ernest Bevin used to call it. But as cricket is a way of life for me, so I feel that the phrase can equally well be applied to life itself. So for those of you who are not cricket fanatics, there is no need to despair. There is more than just cricket in this book, which takes up from where I left off at the end of 1973 in my first autobiography *It's Been A Lot Of Fun*. I only hope that *you* will think that It's *STILL* a Lot of Fun.

St John's Wood
Christmas 1977

First Over 'As I was saying . . .'

It was that great *Daily Mirror* columnist Cassandra who, on restarting his column at the end of the war, began: 'As I was saying when I was so rudely interrupted . . .' I have no such excuse for starting to write another book. Except perhaps for two things. A number of people after reading *It's Been a Lot of Fun* assumed that I had retired. No such luck for the listeners! I *did* retire as a member of the BBC staff in September 1972 but have continued to work as a freelance ever since.

The other thing became obvious to me on 25 January 1975 – that in spite of my career as a broadcaster for thirty years I was still not as well known as I had thought. This was brought home to me when flying back from Australia. Our aircraft had stopped at Bahrain to refuel at about two o'clock in the morning. I was pacing up and down the transit lounge to get a bit of exercise when an Englishman in an elegant overcoat approached me. Why he was wearing an overcoat in Bahrain where the temperature was in the nineties I don't know. Anyway, he came up and said, 'Excuse me, I think I recognise you.'

So I put on what I thought was a friendly smile at that hour of the morning and began to reach for my pen. 'Who do you think I am, then?' I asked him. 'Tell me,' he said, 'did you ever drive a bus in Watford?' I gasped out a firm '*No*,' and he went on, 'Well, you are the dead spit of a chap who did.' With that he turned and walked off without another word. I am convinced he was not joking nor had done it for a bet.

This lack of fame was further emphasised a few months later at Euston Station – of all places. I had come down on the sleeper from Manchester and at 7 am was walking up the cold dark platform, not looking my best I must admit after a night on the train. I heard footsteps behind me, and soon a man drew level with me. He gave me a good hard look then said, 'Do I know you?'

'I don't know,' I replied, 'who *do* you think I am?' 'Aren't you Alan Dixon?' he asked. Well, poor Alan, who was a BBC sports commentator in North Region, had died about six years before. So I said, 'Alan Dixon? But he's dead.' 'Yes,' replied the man. 'I know he is!' To this day I still cannot work out what he meant!

Anyhow, with *Down Your Way* as a weekly basis, life in my 'retirement' in the autumn of 1973 was as busy as ever. I went up to Manchester to record two programmes of *Call My Bluff*, something I had always wanted to do. I was in Paddy Campbell's team and although I did not do too badly, I could not match the skill and ease with which Paddy and Frank Muir played. We recorded the two programmes during the evening in front of the same audience. We changed our ties, shirts and coats before the second one but kept on the same trousers.

I expect that, like me, you imagined that the panel made up their own meanings of the words. This was, I believe, tried originally, but now the *True* or *False* explanations are cleverly composed in advance and typed on to little cards. An hour or so before the show you are 'summoned' to the Captain's dressing-room where, after consultation, he allots you your cards, either *True* or *False*. You then learn these and have them in front of you during the programme. You can vary them to suit your own particular style. Much of the art of winning the game depends on the selection by the Captain of the right person to give the *True* version of a particular word. A deadpan face and the ability to lie convincingly are essential ingredients for the contestants. It's certainly as much fun to do as it is to watch, but alas I have not been asked back (yet!).

In November 1973 the Lord Mayor's Show came round again for TV and this has become a hardy annual ever since. The timing has always been dicey, the ideal being for the Lord Mayor's coach to pass our commentary position opposite St Paul's about a minute before the end of our broadcast.

But this is the longest *unrehearsed* procession in the world and I regret that on two occasions we have missed the Lord Mayor before we had to hand back to the studio. But in 1976 we achieved perfection with the Lord Mayor reaching us on the dot, and what is more, for the first time ever he surprised viewers by speaking a message to them from the window of his coach as it passed our cameras. The secret was that our engineers had been along early to the Mansion House before the Lord Mayor got dressed in all his finery and robes, and had 'wired' him up with a small microphone and pocket transmitter.

I had often been to the Festival of Remembrance at the Royal Albert Hall but 1973 was the first year I had commentated on it for radio. Previously I had resisted doing it as I feel that this service and the Two-minute Silence are very personal matters for people who, like myself, lost many friends during the war. But it went all right – unlike the Two-minute Silence service broadcast once by a West Indian radio station. The programme was being recorded in the main square of the town and at about five minutes to the hour the engineer in the control room sat listening to the hymns and the bands playing. He then unfortunately dozed off, but awoke a few minutes later and to his horror heard nothing coming over the air. Thinking that there had been a breakdown he automatically went into his emergency drill and put on a record of martial music. Result – the Two-minute Silence was shattered. So was the poor engineer when he realised what he had done.

At about this time I was a member of the panel on another sporting quiz, *Sporting Chance*, which is always fun to do and keeps one informed about sports other than cricket. One of my friends who heard the programme was inspired to send me a rude postcard which showed a quiz master putting a question to a panellist.

QUIZ MASTER   What did Eve say to Adam the first time she saw him?
PANELLIST *(After a long pause)* Ah – that's a hard one.
QUIZ MASTER   Quite right – two marks!

In mid-November 1973 there was Princess Anne's wedding

to Captain Mark Phillips and as usual the BBC went to town and pulled out all its ceremonial stops. I had previously been a commentator for TV for King George VI's funeral, the Coronation and Princess Margaret's wedding. But this time I was selected for radio and had a superb position on the corner of the Mall and Horse Guards Parade. I had to describe the procession on its way to and from the Abbey, and also did some interviews with the crowd. I was lucky enough to be one of the few to go to Buckingham Palace the evening before to see the wonderful collection of wedding cakes which had been sent to the Princess. There were dozens of them, many with horsey motifs, and it was nice to learn that they were all being sent off to hospitals. We were also shown the seating plan for the wedding breakfast – round tables for about ten people each – and a preview of the menu and wines. I can assure you they were mouth-watering and I thought of them as I munched a ham sandwich in my car as I rushed off to Shropshire to do a *Down Your Way*.

Our daughter Clare flew back from Australia and we had a very happy family Christmas at our cliff house in Swanage. As usual, all seven of us opened our stockings together early Christmas morning on Pauline's and my bed. I love Christmas but must admit that a well-known vicar got the retort he deserved when he said in his sermon: 'Christmas is a time of great and enduring joy for all of God's two-legged creatures.' One of his parishioners was heard to say in a loud voice, 'Try telling that to a turkey'!

The year 1974 started off with a quick trip to West Germany to record some quizzes with the forces, one of which took place in an RAF hospital. I was told that the Queen Mother had been there six months before and as usual had gone round all the wards talking to the patients. She came to a man who was writhing with pain in his bed. 'What's wrong with you?' she asked sympathetically. 'Oh, Mam,' replied the man, 'I'm in great pain. I've got an awful boil on my bum.' 'Oh dear, very painful,' said the Queen Mum, not batting an eyelid. 'I do hope it gets better soon.'

She passed down the ward and when she had left the sister

came back and gave the man a terrific rocket. 'How dare you mention a word like that to Royalty – or to any visitor for that matter. Make something up. Say you've sprained your ankle. But never use THAT word again.' The man said he was very sorry and quite understood and promised never to do it again.

Three months or so later, Princess Margaret came out to Germany to visit one of the Highland Regiments of which she is Colonel. She came to the same hospital and like her Mother talked to all the men in the wards. Eventually she came to the man with the boil (he was still there), and asked him what was wrong. Remembering the sister's instructions he replied: 'I'm in great pain, Mam. I have a badly sprained ankle.' 'Oh,' said the Princess with some surprise, 'so the boil on your bum is better, is it?'

I hope the story was true. But I doubt it!

Most of January and February 1974 was taken up with launching my autobiography *It's Been a Lot of Fun*, and all the publicity connected with it. Radio did us proud and I appeared on most of the programmes such as *Today*, *Open House*, *Be My Guest*, *Jack de Manio Precisely*, *Desert Island Discs* and quite a bit of local radio round the country. Television was not so generous, only *Pebble Mill* in Birmingham giving me a spot. I had long wanted to receive the accolade of appearing on *Desert Island Discs*, the longest running programme on the BBC. Roy Plomley not only thought up the idea during the war but has presented it ever since, and is a most friendly and sympathetic interviewer. My selection of eight records was a fair reflection of my tastes and was as follows:

1 *Eton Boating Song* sung by Eton College Musical Society
2 *All the things you are* sung by Hutch
3 *We'll gather lilacs* sung by Vanessa Lee and Bruce Trent
4 *Double Damask* A sketch by Cicely Courtneidge
5 *Strolling* sung by Bud Flanagan
6 Elgar's *Enigma Variations* played by Philharmonia Orchestra conducted by Sir Malcolm Sargent
7 *Tie a yellow ribbon round the ole oak tree* sung by Dawn
8 *End of the party* Composed and sung by Barry Alexander (my eldest son so called because there was already another member of Equity named Barry Johnston)

The book I chose to take with me was John Fisher's *Funny Way to be a Hero*. It is an analysis of British Music Hall with biographies and routines of all the great comics and comedy acts.

My book was published in the middle of February 1974 and I'm happy to say received a very kind press. Unfortunately we had to battle with the three-day week and the General Election, so that when the first print sold out there were long delays before more books could be got to the shops. So we lost some of the impetus of the early publicity but in the end my book did quite well and at the final count had sold over fifteen thousand copies. Not in the David Niven class, of course, but not too bad. I suppose I should have put in some of my early sexual experiences, though I'm afraid they would not have been as amusing as his undoubtedly were!

Our publication date was also not too cleverly timed, as the following week Pauline and I flew off to Barbados for a long-planned holiday – thanks to *Down Your Way* allowing me to pre-record three programmes. The main idea was to see the Third Test between England and West Indies at Bridgetown. It was strange to sit in the stand and just watch the cricket *without commentating*. I must confess that at the end of the day I was far more exhausted than if I had been working.

England, already one down in the series, managed to draw the match after being put into bat by Kanhai. They got off to a terrible start but were saved by Greig (148) and Knott (87) who took the score from 130 for 5 to 293 for 6, England finally making 395.

West Indies replied with 596 for 8 declared, of which Lance Rowe made 302, the highest innings by a West Indian batsman against England. It was the third score of over 300 which I had seen in a Test and I must admit I'm not too keen to see another. The other two were 311 by Bobby Simpson at Old Trafford in 1964, and 307 by Bob Cowper at Melbourne in 1966. Rowe's was the most entertaining of the three but however good the batsman, it's rather like a brilliant after-dinner speaker going on too long.

England, thanks to a not out hundred by Keith Fletcher,

drew the game, which was remarkable for the fact that altogether ninety-nine no balls were called – seventy-nine not being scored off by the batsmen. This is a record but not one to be proud of, although of course with the present front foot law it is not as easy as it seems. However, I am always surprised that even the greatest bowlers – including slow ones like Underwood – give so many runs away simply because they fail to put their front foot in the right place during their delivery stride.

This Test was the turning point of the tour for England. They batted well in a rain-spoilt match in Guyana and then went on to win a thrilling game in the Final Test at Port of Spain, winning by 26 runs with one hour to spare, and so squaring the series. It had been a triumph for Dennis Amiss who, in the Tests, scored 663 runs with an average of 82.87 and 3 hundreds. Tony Greig also emerged as a formidable all-rounder with 430 runs and 24 wickets, mostly taken by his off-spin which was helped by the bounce in the wickets.

It was Mike Denness' first tour as captain and he grew in confidence and tactical skills as it progressed. But it was difficult for him initially, as at least six of the players had played in more Tests than he, and naturally he felt he had to make his mark as a leader. He tried to do this by largely going his own way and not often seeking the advice of his more experienced players. But as his confidence grew he became more receptive to their opinions and, in the end, although not up to his best form with the bat, came out of the tour with the credit of having led a happy and not unsuccessful team.

Back in England after three glorious weeks of sunshine, I appeared in Derek Nimmo's chat show, *Just a Nimmo*, which was great fun. The theme of the programme was sporting commentary and the others on the show were Cliff Morgan and Jimmy Hill. I had often seen Derek do his 'toe twiddling' act, which he performed goodness knows how many times during the long run of *Charley Girl*. He had evidently heard that I can tuck my ears in, and quite out of the blue without previous warning, he asked me to do it during the show. So for the first time after nearly thirty years on TV, I tucked my ears in for millions to see. It caused some hilarity and had an amusing sequel a few weeks later.

We were doing a *Down Your Way* in Kirby Lonsdale and had got lost in the dark on our way to interview someone just outside the town. I spotted a lane leading up to a farm, so we drove up and I knocked on the door.

After some delay, a woman came to the door and peered out into the gloom. Her face lit up when she saw me and her first words were: 'Can you really tuck them in?' Only after proving that I could did she say, 'Good Evening, Mr Johnston', and showed us the right way to our prospective victim.

He happened to be a prosperous farmer and as we sat in front of a crackling log fire, I learnt a very good tip from his wife. They had some beautiful carnations in a vase, and when I admired them, she said they were over a fortnight old. I asked her how she kept them so fresh, and she explained that instead of putting them in water, she always used fizzy lemonade. I have tried it ever since and I can assure you it works – they really do stay fresh for far longer.

Incidentally, while recalling the farmer's wife who asked me to tuck in my ears, I couldn't help thinking of the stupid story of a man who also called at a house late one night. He was telling a friend about it and said, 'I knocked and a woman opened the door in her nightdress,' and the friend remarked: 'What a funny place to have a door'!

After commentating on the 1974 Boat Race from Chiswick Bridge for radio, and the Battersea Easter Parade for TV, I introduced a charity concert at Welwyn for my friend Martin Gilliat. It was a serious musical occasion and I was taught an object lesson of when not to try to be funny. The lady accompanying the singers at the piano was a Miss Nunn, and although her name was in the programme I thought I ought to give a verbal credit, so I said: 'And now, ladies and gentlemen, I am sure you would like to show your appreciation of the lady at the piano. Before the show started I was talking to her and asked her what her name was. And answer came there Nunn!' And deservedly, except for a loud guffaw from Martin in the front row, laughter also came there none!

It was a wet summer for the double tour of India and Pakistan. England under Mike Denness beat India easily three–nil and so avenged their defeat at the Oval in 1971. As so often happens over here, the Indian batsmen could not cope with the England fast bowlers and seamers. This time Old, Hendrick, Arnold, Willis and Greig took all the wickets except for four by Underwood, who was the only spinner selected by England for any of the six Tests during the summer. The famous trio of Indian spinners, Bedi, Chandrasekar and Prasanna, came off just as badly and the England batsmen made a packet of runs against them. The England batting averages were remarkable and must be a record for any top six batsmen for any country in a Test series. Here they are:

David Lloyd	260.00
Keith Fletcher	189.00
John Edrich	101.00
Mike Denness	96.33
Dennis Amiss	92.50

and Tony Greig a comparative failure with only 79.50.

Wadekar on his second tour to England as captain had an unhappy time not only as captain but also with the bat. I felt especially sorry for him because, as a leg-puller myself, I appreciated the time he pulled *my* leg in 1967. And what's more he did it in front of the TV cameras.

It happened one Sunday at Southport when BBC 2 was covering a match between the Indians and Lancashire, the Indian tourists including their captain the Nawab of Pataudi and Wadekar himself. I have discovered since that a conspiracy took place between Pataudi and Desmond Smith who was the PRO for Rothmans at the time. They saw that instead of commentating as I usually did, on this particular Sunday I had the job of interviewing batsmen as they returned to the pavilion. It's a dicey job at the best of times as no one who has just been bowled by a full pitch, or caught off a dolly, relishes being asked what happened. You know – ask a silly question . . .

Anyway, I was sitting in a deckchair in front of the pavilion when I saw that Wadekar was out. So I got up and with my microphone went out to meet him. We had become good friends on the tour and I always called him Wadders and he called me Johnners. So it was with some confidence that I approached him and in front of the cameras asked him, 'What happened Wadders?'

Instead of the smile I was expecting I noticed that his face was completely blank, so thinking he had not heard me over the applause of the crowd, I repeated the question. To my utter surprise he said in broken English – 'Sorry, I no speak English, not understand' and continued on his way to the dressing-room. 'But Wadders,' I gasped, 'we've often talked together on the tour – surely you understand. How did you get out?' But it was no good, he brushed me aside murmuring: 'Me no speak English – sorry' and disappeared into the pavilion.

Was my face red as I turned to face the camera! I tried to laugh it off – not very successfully – and hurriedly handed back to the commentator. I wasn't really angry – just embarrassed and nonplussed, but couldn't help laughing when I hurried into the dressing-room to find all the Indians, including Wadekar, in fits of laughter. I had to admit it – in front of several million people I had been well and truly done!

Pakistan were a tougher nut to crack and all three Tests in 1974 were drawn. Rain interfered with the first two at Leeds and Lord's. No play was possible on the fifth day at Headingley with England needing 44 runs to win with 4 wickets in hand, Fletcher being 67 not out and Old not out 10, with Arnold, Underwood and Hendrick to come. It could have been a very close thing either way. At Lord's, Pakistan had all the bad luck with the weather and leaking covers, Underwood having a field day with 13 wickets in the match. But once again there was no play possible on the last day when England only needed 60 to win with all their wickets in hand. So this time it seems certain that *they* would have won.

There was quite a hoo-ha about the covers – or lack of them as the Pakistan manager Omar Kureishi thought. In an official protest he accused MCC of 'an appalling show of negligence and incompetence in not covering the pitch adequately'. Strong words, but as MCC Secretary Jack Bailey pointed out, the slope at Lord's makes it extremely difficult to prevent water from running down from the grandstand side. It's difficult to believe but the level of the boundary at the Tavern side is seven feet lower than the grandstand boundary, a big drop when you consider that the ground is only 144 yards across.

The Third Test at the Oval was a very different affair. The sun shone and both sides made gigantic totals on a slow, easy pitch – Pakistan 600 for 7 declared; and 94–4, England 545. For Pakistan, Zakeer Abbas, spectacles gleaming in the sunlight, played superbly for his 240, his first Test hundred since his 274 on his Test debut against England at Edgbaston in 1971. For England, Amiss scored his eighth Test hundred and as usual did not give up after reaching three figures, going on to make 183. Both he and Fletcher had a splendid summer but with the Australian tour coming up the England batting still lacked a consistently successful opening pair. They were far too liable to early collapses with someone like Knott or Old having to come to the rescue later on.

We had our usual number of amusing incidents in the commentary box. In the First Test against India at Old Trafford there was no play on the Saturday until 1 pm. I was due to begin the commentary at 11.30 am when play should have started. But it was a cold miserable day with rain and dark clouds, and the Indian spectators were sitting miserably huddled together in one of the stands. I heard my cue from Radio 3 in my headphones '. . . and so to find out the prospects of play, over to Brian Johnston at Old Trafford'.

'It's raining here,' I said, 'and there certainly won't be any play for some time yet.' I then meant to say, 'There's a dirty black *cloud* here.' Unfortunately, what I *did* say was, 'There's a dirty black *crowd* here!' Collapse of everyone in the box, including the former Maharajah of Baroda – or Prince as we called him – who was one of our summarisers throughout the series.

Then, during the Second Test at Lord's against Pakistan we pulled off a leg-pull on Henry Blofeld. There were a lot of interruptions for rain on the Saturday, and whenever it does rain we do our best not to return to the studio for music. Instead we try to fill in the time by answering listeners' letters, interviewing people or just discussing current cricket topics. We were doing just that early in the afternoon when there was no play. We were all in the box and took it in turns to introduce some new subject.

Henry – who when he gets excited talks very fast and hardly draws breath – got stuck into some topic in which he was passionately interested. Looking straight into the microphone he talked at a great pace completely ignoring the rest of us. After two or three minutes he still had not brought any of us into the discussion. So we all quietly left our seats and got our producer Peter Baxter to slip a note in front of Henry. All it said was, 'Keep going until 6.30 pm!'

This momentarily stopped Henry in his tracks. You should have seen his face as he saw the rain pouring down outside with little prospect of play, and realised that we had all deserted him. But he carried on gamely, and we soon had mercy on him, and slipped back into our seats . . .

Second Over 'A life full of moment'

During my September 1974 holiday in Swanage I caught a bug – and still have it. Golf. As a boy I had played the occasional nine holes with my old Mum, but never seriously. Most of my shots sailed over extra cover with the usual cricketer's slice. After that, with a family of five and generally working for the BBC every Saturday and some Sundays, I never seemed to have any spare time. Whenever I did, in the summer I played cricket, and in the winters on tours with MCC was quite happy to go to the beaches.

I am a very bad golf player, and still have no handicap except for my slice and my swing. But my friends have been incredibly kind and patient, and allow me to play with them: we normally play a greensome in which all four of us drive off and then each partnership chooses which of their drives they wish to play. This is not always the longest drive, as if mine has gone a reasonable distance and is fairly straight, it is good tactics for my partner to play the second shot. In this way a bad player like myself can have some slight influence on the result of a game. But with a four-ball I trail miserably behind, and it virtually becomes my partner versus our opponents.

I have worked out my own philosophy of golf. During a round – if lucky I may play as many as six reasonably good shots. Afterwards it is these that I cherish and remember and forget all about the many bad ones. My friends on the other hand are all pretty good average golfers. So they play many good shots and only a few bad ones. But judging from their conversation it is these latter that they remember and worry about, so that I often end up happier than they do.

Now that I play I appreciate golf on TV all the more and

try to discover its secrets by watching the masters. I am encouraged to see that even they play a few slices or hooks, but am immediately depressed by the ease with which they invariably get out of trouble. Mind you, they do have one advantage over me. When *they* slice, the ball often hits the long line of spectators, and bounces back on to the fairway. But nobody comes to watch *me*, so that my slice disappears into impenetrable undergrowth.

Inevitably I suppose, I have begun to collect golf stories which make a change from cricket. It's interesting that quite a few of them have to do with death, starting with that oldest of chestnuts:

Two golfers were putting on a green by a road, when a funeral procession went slowly by. One of the players took off his cap and stood reverently to attention. His opponent remarked on this unusual display of respect for the dead person. 'Well,' said the player, 'it's the least I can do. I was married to her for forty years.'

Then there was the very bad golfer with a terrible slice which always went into the rough. When he died his will requested that his ashes be scattered on the fifteenth fairway. So after his funeral his friends took the urn up to the course and as requested emptied it out on to the fifteenth fairway. But unfortunately a strong wind was blowing and blew the ashes straight into the rough!

There was also the elderly golfer who was worried whether he would get any golf when he died and went to heaven. So he found a crystal gazer and asked him about the prospects for golf in the after-life. The crystal gazer looked into his crystal ball for a few moments and then announced that he had two bits of news, one good, one bad. The golfer asked for the good news first. The crystal gazer told him he could see a beautifully laid out course with perfect fairways and smooth lush greens. The golfer was delighted but said he supposed he had better hear the bad news, too. 'Here it is,' said the crystal gazer. 'I am sorry to tell you that I can see you driving off the first tee at 9.30 am next Thursday!'

On a slightly more corny note there was the golfer who always carried a spare pair of socks in his bag – just in case he ever got a hole in one.

And then there was the long driver of the ball who regularly hit it two hundred and fifty yards or more. But gradually over a period of a few months he found that he was beginning to hit the ball shorter and shorter distances. From two hundred and fifty yards he went down to two hundred and twenty-five, then to two hundred, and a hundred and fifty until in the end he couldn't hit it more than a hundred yards. So he decided to go to his doctor to find out if there was anything wrong with his health. The doctor examined him thoroughly and then told him he had two things to tell him, one good, one bad. 'Let's have the bad first,' said the golfer. 'Okay,' said the doctor, 'stand by for a shock. You are gradually changing into a woman.' The golfer turned pale and croaked out, 'Come on, quick, give me the good news.' 'Right-ho,' said the doctor, 'from now on you'll be able to drive from the ladies' tees!'

Jimmy Tarbuck tells a lovely story of the golfer who was always accompanied by his dog when playing a round. Every time the golfer made a good shot or sank a long putt, the dog would stand up on his hind legs and applaud his master with his front paws. A friend asked him what the dog did when the golfer landed in a bunker or missed an easy putt. 'Oh,' said the golfer, 'he turns somersaults.' 'How many?' asked the friend. 'It depends on how hard I kick him up the arse,' was the reply.

And finally what about the unorthodox golfer who, like Brian Close, could play equally well either right- or left-handed. His opponents never knew which it would be until he drove off from the first tee. One of them asked him how he decided which way he would play. He replied that if, when he woke up in the morning, his wife was lying on her right side, then he would play right-handed. If she was lying on her left side, then he played left-handed. 'But what happens if she is lying on her back?' asked the opponent. 'In that case,' said the man, 'I ring up the club to say I will be an hour late!'

In between learning golf my September holiday was twice interrupted. First I went to Manchester to record *Reunion* for BBC TV. This was a series where three people who had been at school together met to discuss their schooldays and the paths which their lives had taken since then. My old school chums were William Douglas-Home and Jo Grimond. We had been at Eton and Oxford together and before the war had occupied the same house at 35, South Eaton Place. It was kept by a lovely couple called Mr and Mrs Crisp. Since then, William had become one of our most popular and prolific playwrights with an unerring touch for dialogue and light comedy. At the time of our recording he had had sixteen plays in the West End averaging three hundred and fifty performances each – not bad! Jo had been leader of the Liberal party from 1956–1967 and was – and still is – the father figure of that party. M⁻ favourite remark by a Liberal was attributed to that gre⸴ character Lady Asquith. When asked what she thought of the two-chamber system she is said to have replied: 'I personally couldn't do without it. You see, my husband is a liberal peer.'

Anyway, under the tactful and friendly chairmanship of Brian Redhead, William, Jo and I were given our heads and encouraged to talk non-stop for about forty minutes – not something which any of us found very difficult to do! But somehow we each managed to get a fair share of the conversation. We came to no very profound conclusions except that Eton was the best trades union in the world and that all three of us had been very lucky in the jobs we had chosen to do.

Towards the end of September 1974 I flew off to South Africa for a week as I had been asked to share the commentary with my old friend Charles Fortune on the Datsun International Double Wicket Competition. I wonder what Lord Harris would have had to say about a Japanese car firm sponsoring cricket matches! Anyway, it is a splendid form of cricket consisting of two-a-side, with a maximum of 8 overs an innings – and each team playing the others once in a one-innings match.

It must have been an eye-opener to those who still belittle what South Africa is doing to try to integrate her sport – especially cricket. There in Johannesburg playing together, staying in the same hotels, attending receptions together, and sharing dressing-rooms were teams from South Africa white, South Africa black, England, Australia,

New Zealand, West Indies and Pakistan. They were all perfectly happy and thoroughly enjoyed the experience, which of course would not have been possible a year or two earlier.

The big crowds enjoyed it too, especially as Eddie Barlow and Barry Richards won it for South Africa white, but only after a tough fight against South Africa black. What a turn-up for the books that would have been had the latter won. But the success of the competition bore out what I have always felt. It is grossly unfair to punish cricketers for apartheid by cancelling their tours, and with boycotts and demonstrations. It is not *their* fault. Blame the politicians but leave sport alone. In the end I am sure it will be the best means of achieving unity between whites, coloureds and blacks – all over the world.

In October I was paid a wonderful and much appreciated compliment by those friendly and generous cricket fanatics – The Wombwell Cricket Lovers Society. They gave a special dinner in my honour and presented me with the 1974 Denzil Batchelor Memorial Award for 'Services to Cricket'. It was totally undeserved because, as I have said so often, I have been lucky enough to earn my living from what is really my life's hobby. But it was a delightful occasion with some excellent speeches by the Bishop of Wakefield and the President of Yorkshire, Sir Kenneth Parkinson.

I have known the latter since before the war, when on my various visits to Yorkshire he used to entertain us at parties with his conjuring tricks. He tells an amusing story of how as an average club cricketer he was called on to open the batting to that very fast bowler the late Father R. P. H. Uttley of Hampshire. Both the first two balls which he received pitched on his middle and leg, and with a loud click the balls shot off to the fine leg boundary. On each occasion there were loud appeals for LBW, but the pace was a bit too fast for the elderly umpire to follow the ball. So hearing the sound of a ball on wood he signalled a four to the batsman each time. A few balls later a very fast yorker from Uttley spreadeagled Kenneth's stumps, and he retired to the pavilion to considerable applause for those two finely executed leg-glides. How was the umpire, or the unsuspecting crowd, to know that Kenneth had a *wooden* left leg which now had two large dents on it the size of a cricket ball!

This reminds me of the batsman who *did* glide a ball off his legs down to long leg. But the bowler appealed for LBW, and when the batsman trotted confidently down to the other end, he saw to his horror that the umpire's finger was up. 'You can't give me out LBW,' he said, 'I hit that ball hard.' 'I know you did,' said the umpire thinking quickly, 'I am merely signalling byes.'

My health at the dinner was proposed by Trevor Bailey, who over the past few years has added much wisdom and caustic wit to our ball by ball commentaries. He tells a splendid story against himself. In 1954 in the First Test at Brisbane, Australia were put in to bat by Len Hutton. They had scored about 300 for 2 when Trevor came on for a final spell. Hot and tired, he ran up to bowl but the ball stuck in his hand so that although he went through his bowling action, he did not actually deliver the ball. 'That's the best bloody ball you've bowled today, Biley!' shouted a barracker.

Anyway, the dinner was a lovely occasion for me, and Les Bailey, the Society's Poet Laureate, wrote these kind words on the back of the menu.

A life full of moment, bonhomie and cheer
From Eton to Oxford to a young Grenadier.
BBC Outside Broadcasts and pastures quite new
Where he even survived being once sawn in two.
Now a rich sense of humour, an eloquent style
Has added to cricket a reason to smile.
And all the world over where the great game is played
The sunshine of commentary is the memory he made.
At Cricket, Monte Carlo, or just Down Your Way
We'll remember him always – till the last close of play.

In December 1974 we had a rather unique gathering of past and present Grenadiers – officers and senior NCO's – to say goodbye and thank you to our much loved Colonel of the Regiment, General Sir Allan Adair. It took the form of a mixed cocktail party in the Banqueting Hall in Whitehall, and there must have been at least a thousand people present. So as you can imagine, there were plenty of reminiscences!

Among these was the tale of a very gallant and distinguished ex-officer who had won the Victoria Cross in Italy. A friend of mine who served with him out there was censoring the letters of the men in his company and one of them wrote: 'Captain —— has just been awarded the Victoria Cross. If he was as bloody to the Germans as he is to us he thoroughly deserves it. P.S. Let them keep their f . . . . . . medals. The only cross I want to see is Charing Cross!' When my friend finished this story someone else asked if we knew that old Major X (a very ugly officer) had been attached to the French in 1940, and had done so well that he was recommended for the Croix de Guerre. Unfortunately they couldn't find a French General who was prepared to kiss him!

But the star of the party was Mr Harold Macmillan, who had served with the Regiment in France during the Great War. He made an excellent speech in praise of Sir Allan and told this story about the war in the trenches.

He and some other officers were sitting in a dug-out near the front line. They were drinking port although their Commanding Officer, Colonel 'Ma' Jeffries, strongly disapproved of drinking and discouraged them from doing so. They had several bottles open on a wooden table when to their dismay they heard footsteps approaching along the trench, and by the voices realised it was the Commanding Officer making an inspection. They hurriedly got some candles, stuck them in the half-filled bottles, and managed to light them just before 'Ma' Jeffries entered the dug-out. They all got up and stood to attention, and the Colonel seemed quite pleased with all he saw, and after a short chat went on his way. Much relieved, they quickly removed the candles and went on with their drinking.

About six months later one of them met Colonel Jeffries in the Guards Club in London. 'Would you like a glass of port, Colonel?' asked the officer. 'I think I'd prefer a small brandy if I may,' replied the Colonel. 'The port might taste of wax.' I was lucky enough to be introduced to Mr Macmillan later in the evening and he assured me that the story was true.

But I didn't dare ask about the one told me about him by Lord Carrington, who was in the 2nd Battalion Grenadier

Guards with me throughout the war. He was known as 'the small peer', and behind his spectacles and mild expression, he's a very determined character. Not only is he extremely brave and strong-minded but also has a lot of talent, something a stranger would never suspect on first meeting him. It was his platoon of Sherman tanks who took Nijmegen Bridge in Holland in September 1944 and for which action he was awarded the MC. In addition to his political career in this country he was possibly the ablest and most popular High Commissioner Britain has ever had in Australia. He has a wonderful sense of humour and was highly respected by everyone in Australia. I think it's no secret that they would have liked him to be their Governor-General, but it would have meant his being away for five years from the centre of the political scene, and would also have involved a large financial sacrifice.

Anyhow, he told me this story of Mr Macmillan who visited Australia on a Commonwealth tour during the peak time of his 'Super Mac' reign as Prime Minister. He was given a great welcome wherever he went by British immigrants who gathered at airports or outside his hotels to see and cheer him. He sensed their homesickness and desire for news from home, so made a habit of giving a little speech which always started with the phrase, 'I bring you greetings from the Old Country'. He did this hundreds of times, always accompanying it with a little circular wave of the right hand.

One day, he and Lord Carrington were sitting in the back of a car on their way to some place in the outback, miles from anywhere, and passing through desolate countryside. They were naturally discussing political business as they made their way along the dusty road. Every half-mile or so Mr Macmillan would break off the conversation and wave out of the window with his right hand and mutter, 'I bring you greetings from the Old Country . . . !' his only audience being the odd kangaroo or wombat! I told you that Lord Carrington had a sense of humour!

I had a bit of bad luck myself over the question of drinking in the Grenadiers. When I first joined the 2nd Battalion at Shaftesbury in June 1940 I took with me a dozen bottles of

Perrier-Jouet champagne, as I thought I might as well drink it while the going was good. I put it in charge of the mess-sergeant and thought no more about it. One evening one of the officers who had just returned from Dunkirk decided to throw a birthday party and asked one of the mess-waiters to bring in some champagne. This he did, and everyone including myself drank large quantities of it and remarked on its excellent quality – far better than the usual cheap brand we usually had. It soon ran out and yes, you've guessed it. It was *my* precious case which we had been drinking, as revealed by an apologetic mess-sergeant when he returned from an evening out.

Even in retirement I still seemed to be flying all over the world, and after Christmas and New Year's Eve in St John's Wood, I flew off to Australia on the first day of 1975. The excuse was to try and push sales of my book in Australia but I must admit that the main reason was to see another Test at my second favourite cricket ground, Sydney (Lord's must be No. 1). Christopher Martin-Jenkins was now the official BBC Cricket Correspondent and so was covering all MCC tours as I had in the past. So it was just a holiday for me and we pre-recorded three *Down Your Ways* to enable me to be away for nearly four weeks.

While in Australia I appeared on quite a few TV and radio chat shows to talk about the book plus some fruitful interviews with the Press. I stayed with my daughter Clare in a house she shared with some other girls in the pleasant Woollahra district of Sydney. As usual I had a marvellous time with lots of parties, bathing, harbour cruises and trips up country.

Clare and I gave a small party at her house for friends and some of the MCC party and their wives. We adjudged it to have been an unqualified success when in the early hours of the morning the distinguished cricket correspondent of a top London daily bade us goodbye and instead of leaving by the front door, tottered up the stairs and disappeared into a cupboard!

When I arrived the tour was not going well for Mike Denness and his team. They were having a torrid time against the tremendous pace of Lillee and Thomson. They had lost the first two Tests at Brisbane and Perth, but had managed to draw the third at Melbourne thanks to a great innings of 90 by Amiss, some fine fast bowling by Willis and the usual good-all-round performance by Greig. It was in fact a most exciting low-scoring match with Australia eight runs short of victory with two wickets standing, and England might well have won it had Hendrick not pulled a hamstring after bowling only fourteen balls in Australia's first innings.

Poor Mike Denness was getting the blame for everything and with Test scores of 6, 27, 2, 20, 8, 2, he decided to drop himself for the Sydney Test. But to be fair he was not the only one who was failing, and after seeing Lillie and Thomson bowl at Sydney I was convinced that no team in the world – not even the South African or West Indies stars – would have done any better. This was borne out the following year when the West Indies lost five of their Tests.

The Australian opening pair made a fearsome sight. At one end there was the long classical run up and action, the speed, accuracy and variations in pace of Lillee. At the other the thunderbolts of Thomson delivered off a shortish run with a slinging action and the right arm coming over *at the very last moment* from right behind his back. Much of his lightning speed was generated by his tremendously powerful shoulders. The Sydney pitch had pace, and even more important, bounce. They did not *have* to bowl short to get the ball to rise, though of course they unleashed a number of bouncers, one or two from Thomson soaring over Marsh's head, although he was standing at least twenty-five yards back. A good length ball from them was sufficient to force the batsmen to play almost every stroke chest or head high. Batting became a matter of self-preservation.

It might have been possible just to stay there by ducking and swaying out of the way. But runs had to be scored *somehow*. It was all very well for the critics from the safety of the stands to say 'get behind the line of the ball'. But what in fact could this have achieved? What scoring stroke *can* you play against a good length ball coming straight at your head if you are dead in line? So the temptation was to try the occasional injudicious hook or to run or steer the ball towards third man, sometimes deliberately over the slips, with body well away from the bat. Remember that in 1932–3 the great Don Bradman had the skill and quickness of eye and foot to step back towards square leg and play Larwood's leg-side attack into the vacant spaces on the off-side. He was heavily criticised at the time for doing so, but managed to score 396 runs and average 56.57 in the series, though of course for him this was comparative failure.

In spite of everything, England nearly saved this Sydney Test thanks to some typically plucky batting by John Edrich, who after a sickening blow from one of the few balls that didn't rise went off to hospital. But he returned to block for two and a half hours and made 33 not out. Due to him and the tail-enders Willis and Arnold, there were only five overs and three balls left when Australia won, and so regained the Ashes which had been won by Ray Illingworth's side on the same ground four years before.

Remarkably, a record Sydney crowd of 178,027 watched the match. I say remarkably because just as this type of blistering attack is dangerous and unpleasant for batsmen, it is also unpleasant and boring for the cricket-loving spectator. No one, except those who would have got a kick out of the gladiators of ancient Rome, can really enjoy watching batsmen literally fighting for their lives or at best preventing serious injury.

An even worse effect is that it limits the number of strokes which it is *possible* to play in front of the wicket, however good the batsman may be. In this match for Australia, there was a classic 144 by Greg Chappell and some solid batting by McCosker (80) and Redpath (105). And for England there was just one innings which the connoisseur of stroke play could appreciate. That was an astonishing 82 by Alan Knott who played every known stroke in the book and a good many which are not and never will be in it! He is a wonderful improviser on the basis of a sound technique, and on this occasion, he slashed, lashed, hooked, dabbed, steered, glided, cut, drove and any other word you can think of ! He played with such success that he actually made 56 in an hour after lunch off his own bat – amazing going against that pace and the inevitable slow over-rate.

Final proof for me of the pace of Lillee and Thomson were

the hands of Rodney Marsh. He showed them to me and they were puffy and badly bruised. To protect them he had wound bits of plaster round each finger. I told him it reminded me of an old BBC radio show – *Much Binding ON the Marsh!* Unfortunately he had never heard of Kenneth Horne and Dicky Murdoch's show, so my joke (?) fell a bit flat!

Incidentally, if any young wicket-keeper finds that his hands are getting bruised, I strongly recommend something which I always used, and I'm glad to say Alan Knott does as well today. Place a thin layer of plasticine inside the inner gloves. It's amazing how it helps to absorb the shock of the ball thudding into the gloves. But I *don't* recommend the method used by George Duckworth when his hands took such a battering standing up to Maurice Tate on the fast Australian pitches of his day. He placed a thick piece of raw steak inside his gloves, and as you can imagine, at the end of a long hot day in the field, he was given a wide berth by his team-mates in the dressing-room!

I was back in England when Mike Denness led his side to victory in the final Test at Melbourne, and was delighted for his sake that he made his highest first-class score – 188. Admittedly Thomson was not playing and Lillee only bowled 6 overs because of an injured foot. But losing the series 1–4 was better than at one time looked likely.

Nowadays on tour MCC travel mostly by plane with the occasional coach journey to an up-country match. They rarely if ever go by train, unlike the old days, when they used to travel right across Australia for days on end. The trains even had a lounge with a piano to help while away the time. I don't know any modern player who plays the piano but in the past Ewart Astill of Leicestershire and Dick Pollard of Lancashire were expert ticklers of the ivories, as of course was Don Bradman. He even made a gramophone record when he was over here in 1930. It may also surprise some people to know that that man with flair for so many things – Ted Dexter – plays the organ and piano extremely well. The Warden of Radley College once told me that often after scoring one of his many brilliant hundreds for the school, Ted would take off his pads and relax by going across to the chapel to play a few fugues!

But back to the trains – because there has long been a story told about an MCC player on tour, though no one seems to know for certain which player it really is. I have heard it told about at least half a dozen. Anyway, let's call him Smith and what is said to have happened is this. A girl was nursing a baby in a carriage, the only other occupant of which was a man who kept staring at the baby. He couldn't take his eyes off it, and the girl became more and more embarrassed and annoyed. Finally she could stand it no longer and asked the man why he was staring so. He replied that he would rather not say. But when the girl persisted he said he was sorry but he was staring because the baby was the ugliest which he had ever seen in his life. This naturally upset the girl who broke into floods of tears and taking the baby went and stood in the corridor.

She was still crying when the MCC team came along the corridor on their way to the restaurant car. They all passed her except Smith, who being a decent chap, stopped to ask her why she was crying. She told him that she had just been insulted by a man in her carriage. So Smith said: 'Well, cheer up. I'll bring you back a cup of tea from the restaurant car. That should make you feel better.' So off he went and returned in about five minutes. 'Here's your cup of tea,' he said to the girl, 'and what's more I've also brought a banana for the monkey!' What happened then is not related!

While in Sydney I discovered an interesting story about women's cricket from my daughter, Clare, who was working as sales representative for the New Caledonian Tourist Office in Australia and New Zealand. New Caledonia lies 1,150 miles in the Pacific north-east of Sydney and, said Clare's brochure '. . . is a tropical paradise of blue waters, white sands and lazy hot days and balmy evenings'! Captain Cook found and named New Caledonia in 1774. By 1853 it had become a small French colony and in 1946 was promoted to be a French overseas territory.

The brochure goes on to reveal that 'cricket is played on this small piece of the south of France with the flavour of Paris'. That is unexpected enough. But it becomes even more remarkable when one learns that only WOMEN play. The reason for this seems obscure. It could be that the men consider it too 'cissy' but seeing the tough way in which the women play, that seems unlikely. What *is* certain is that cricket was started by English missionaries in the nineteenth century and that there are now fourteen teams in the capital, Noumea, and three from the adjoining groups of islands, Ouvea, Mare and Lifou. These teams play for a cup awarded annually on 24 September – the anniversary of French occupation – and they practise every Saturday 'with ardour'.

Although the laws and conditions are somewhat eccentric, to say the least, the game is definitely recognisable as cricket, and bears no relation to the French cricket which we all used to play as children. The matches take place on any available land, but usually on a slag pitch, because any grass is reserved for baseball and football. The pitch is sixty-two feet long, the stumps twenty-seven and a half inches high and there are no bails (our pitches are sixty-six feet and the stumps are twenty-eight inches high). Instead of our bowling and popping creases there is a three and a quarter foot square marked out around the stumps in which the batswoman or 'joyeuse' must stand. The bat can be thirty-nine inches long (our maximum is thirty-eight inches) and only three inches wide (ours is four and a quarter inches). So it looks rather like a baseball bat and can be of any weight. The ball – called *'la boule'* – is made of dried sap and bounces, even on a slag pitch. The bowling actions vary from a blatant chuck to a good old-fashioned lob.

The ladies are dressed in gaily-coloured floral smocks called Mother Hubbards – possibly because they are bare underneath! They wear no pads, batting gloves, thigh pads or indeed any other sort of protection so far as can be seen under the smocks. Runs count as in our cricket but are called *'pines'*. There are no boundaries and the batswomen must run up and down the pitch barefoot until the ball is returned to the wicket-keeper. It is therefore not surprising that the laws allow a 'tired' batswoman to be replaced by the next on the list, or to call for a substitute to run for her. Each run is greeted by shrill tin whistles and a hand-clapping version of the Melanesian Pilou-Pilou war song.

The bat must rest on the shoulder and it is forbidden to

hold it in the air or to let it touch the ground. If a player drops the bat she must stay in the square until given another one. Incredibly there is only one ball per over, so there is no over-rate problem in New Caledonia!

And now, in case the whole thing smacks of women's lib, here comes the rub. Both the umpires and the scorer must be MALE. They are considered to be fairer and to have more authority in a dispute, and more capable of breaking up a scrap when the women get excited and fight – as they often do. Here are one or two of the laws these male umpires must enforce.

It is forbidden for players to throw insults (modern Test players please note), nor must any player enter the field in a state of drunkenness. And here is something which might well be introduced to Test Cricket – the umpire has the right to send a player off after a warning. Finally, further proof that the males are really in complete charge of the game – neither the players nor the spectators are allowed to look at the score until the game is over. There are no time limits and the game goes on until the umpire declares one side the winner. The losers then have to fork out about five pounds to give to the winners.

So far our women cricketers have never visited New Caledonia, but I know that Rachel Heyhoe-Flint would just love to take on these besmocked Amazons!

Third Over Down YOUR Way

As soon as I had returned to England at the end of January 1975, I began to hear rumours within the BBC that *Down Your Way* (from now on *DYW*) was to be taken off the air. For reasons of economy the BBC were having to make cuts and this meant that Radios 3 and 4 and Radios 1 and 2 would have to share programmes at certain times of the day. So something had to go, and it was no secret that Tony Witby, controller of Radio 4, did not wish to lose a particular favourite of his called *Celebration*. He looked at the tempting time of 5.15 pm on Sundays and decided that it was the right slot for his programme, and that *DYW* would have to be sacrificed.

The news was officially broken to me by producer Richard Burwood as he and I travelled by car during a *DYW* at Sedgefield in County Durham. Even though I had been forewarned, now that it was definite it came as a bit of a shock. The weekly commitment had become very much part of my life.

The news was given to the Press the following week and I must say they really went to town on our behalf. For a thirty-year-old steam radio programme to hit the headlines in this telly age was a rare and unexpected event. There really was a tremendous outcry against the decision. Somehow the BBC had underestimated the affection with which the programme was held. Not only the nationals but all the provincial papers led the protests and the BBC itself was inundated with letters and phone calls from many devoted followers. The director-general, Sir Charles Curran, was brought into it when on a phone-in he turned down the suggestion that *DYW* should continue but be presented by the twenty local BBC radio stations.

The real reason for taking it off was never given officially, except to say it was for economy. Some of the Press took this to mean that the programme itself was too expensive, with a producer, engineer and myself travelling to places all over the country every week. But in terms of cost per minute this made no sense at all. With the repeat on Tuesdays, Radio 4 was getting eighty minutes of air time for about a hundred and thirty pounds – mere chicken-feed compared with most other similar programmes. In fact, when I read it I immediately told my bosses that I would take a cut in my fee if it would be of any help. But they refused to accept this offer and confirmed to me that there was no question of the programme itself being too extravagant or expensive.

The protests continued to pour in – I admit to soliciting a sister, a brother, an elderly aunt and a couple of cousins! – and some of the letters we received were most touching and rewarding. Many felt they were about to lose an old friend and it was nice to have such proof that we evidently provided some innocent pleasure for so many thousands of people.

Quite a few letters of protest were sent to the newspapers and one of the very nicest was written to the *Daily Mail* by comedian Norman Vaughan. He wrote: 'I don't mind things being changed so long as they remain as good or better than they were before. But *Down Your Way* was as gentle and honest as Sunday cricket on the village green.' Alongside that letter was one from another comedian and friend of mine – Dickie Henderson: 'I'm all for change, but why change something which is successful? I found *Down Your Way* not only interesting but educational.' Gentle, honest, interesting, educational – four very welcome adjectives to have applied to our programme.

The last programme was to come from Painswick in Gloucestershire on Sunday, 20 April, but even before then the planners had gone some way to mollify the protestors. It was announced that *DYW* would return temporarily for six programmes on Saturdays in July/August during the usual repeat time of *Any Questions* which was taking its annual six weeks' holiday. But unknown to us even more was going on behind the scenes. The pressure from listeners had impressed Clare Lawson-Dick, the new controller of Radio 4. The first I heard about it was a telephone call from Anthony Smith, the BBC's radio outside producer from Bristol. I knew him well as I had worked with him for many years contributing cricket reports into his Saturday night sports programme from West Region. I was surprised and delighted with what he had to tell me. He said he had just been stopped in a corridor by his immediate boss Michael Bowen, of *Any Questions* fame. Michael had asked Tony whether he would like to produce *DYW*, which was coming back in October on the same regular basis as before, but would in future be produced and run from Bristol. Tony had rung me immediately before I heard it from anyone else, as he wanted to assure me that I would still be the presenter – which was very thoughtful of him.

The announcement in the Press came a month later – appropriately on my birthday, 24 June. In a statement Clare Lawson-Dick said: 'Fans of the programme wrote to us in large numbers asking for it to be restored. We were also greatly touched and influenced by letters from blind and disabled people who were unable to travel and said that *Down Your Way* had been their only means of getting to know Britain.' I think the BBC deserves credit for admitting that their previous decision had been wrong. By so doing they showed that they *do* try to give listeners what they want. It was quite an exercise for the Press office who told me that it was the first time that the BBC had *publicly* admitted to bowing to public pressure on behalf of a programme.

But amidst all our jubilation there was one person in particular for whom I felt very sorry – Phyllis Robinson. With Richard Burwood she had produced the programme from London for the past thirteen years. It had become very much her 'baby' and part of her life, since her associations with it started far earlier than that.

DYW began in December 1946, produced by Leslie Perowne and John Shuter, with boxing and ice hockey commentator Stewart Macpherson as the presenter. The very first one came from Lambeth Walk and for the first ten programmes it came from various parts of London. It was all very free and easy with no preliminary research. Stewart just went along with a recording car, knocked on people's doors and interviewed them there and then. It was naturally very much hit and miss in more senses than one. Not only did Stewart have no prior knowledge of the person he was going to interview, but on one occasion he was actually hit under the chin by a man who came to the door and mistook Stewart for someone who had been molesting his wife! Shortly after this Stewart said he had had enough and that he felt that the programme wasn't 'him'.

Lionel Gamlin then took over for half a dozen programmes until the BBC found that one of their war-time reporters was 'available'. In fact he was virtually unemployed. So they booked him in the early spring of 1947 for a trial six programmes. His name was Richard Dimbleby and he (naturally!) did so well that he continued to do it till 1953, when after exactly three hundred and fifty editions he found that his family newspaper at Richmond, and his growing TV work, made the weekly *DYW* assignment too much of a burden. Phyllis Robinson had started with him as a recorded programme assistant, and then took over as producer towards the end of Richard's time. In those days the programme was occasionally done 'live' from places like the Hebrides, Shetland Islands and the Channel Islands. During the six years Richard only missed one programme when he caught chicken-pox from his eldest son David and then Wynford Vaughan-Thomas deputised for him. He did however have to link the two hundred and fiftieth from his Surrey home because he had broken a rib falling off his horse.

For some reason *DYW* was rested for two years but returned in 1955 with Franklin Englemann (Jingle) to present it. Previously all the interviews had been recorded on to discs but now the era of the tapes had arrived and they have been used ever since. The first of the new *DYW*'s came from Crewe – the theme being all change, with Richard making a typical gesture by going up to Crewe to introduce Jingle. From then on Jingle became *DYW*, and *DYW* became Jingle. People will always associate his strong but friendly personality with the programme. Like Richard, he only missed one between 1955 and 1972. He caught 'flu and as it was coming from Cardiff, Alun Williams was able to deputise for him at the last moment.

Jingle had just recorded his seven hundred and thirty-third programme when he died suddenly in March 1972 and I had to take over from him at short notice, and except for two breaks have done it ever since. As this book goes to press I am 255 not out. The two breaks were during the summer of 1972 when because of my duties as BBC cricket correspondent Roy Trevivian, Geoffrey Wheeler, Alex Macintosh and Paddy Feeney took over for four weeks each. The other was for four weeks in January 1973 when I went to South Africa as PRO for Derrick Robins on his cricket tour out there. My place was taken by that fact-seeking Scotsman with the querulous plaintive voice – Fyfe Robertson – a complete contrast to me in accent and pace of delivery.

The format of *DYW* has changed from time to time, but has always had the basic idea of a certain number of people being interviewed about their town or village and then each being asked to choose a piece of music. For the first two years after Jingle took over it only ran for six months each year, but then settled down to a steady pattern of ten months a year, with Jingle doing *Holiday Hour* in January and February. For ten years the programme lasted for an hour with nine people being interviewed. But ever since I have been the presenter it has lasted for forty minutes with six interviews. In Richard's day the emphasis was very much on the music with short interviews but ever since Jingle took over the interview has invariably been longer than the music. Nowadays the average is something like four and a half minutes of interview and two and a quarter minutes of music.

The choice of music is left entirely up to the person interviewed, with two provisos. It must not have been chosen the week before and obviously it has to be available – either in the BBC Record Library or obtainable in the shops, or perhaps the person interviewed has a private recording. At one time, because the programme goes out first on a Sunday, much sacred music was chosen especially in Scotland. I think people possibly thought that this type of music was what the BBC wanted them to choose. Though there *was* proof in 1958 that even in London the Sunday Puritan spirit still existed. When *DYW* visited Oxford Street the proprietor of an umbrella shop forbade any of his staff to take part because it *did* go out on a Sunday.

Over the years the choice has broadened. Although we still get the inevitable favourites, nowadays we do have a few requests for something in 'the charts'. But there *are* some regulars which continually crop up. In Richard's day it was *Bless this House* and *Now is the Hour*. With Jingle, *Jerusalem* and *Stranger on the Shore* were top favourites. Among our most popular ones today are Handel's *Hallelujah Chorus*, Verdi's *Hebrew Slaves Chorus*, the theme tunes from *Love Story*, *Dr Zhivago* and *The Onedin Line*, and the music from Gilbert and Sullivan. And of course there's our distinctive signature tune which most people know so well but of which they frequently ask the title. It's *Horse-Guards Whitehall*, by Haydn Wood played by the Queen's Hall Light Orchestra.

People also often ask us how we choose the places which we visit. As we are now approaching our fourteen hundredth town and village, this is getting a little bit harder every year. Stick a pin in a map of the United Kingdom to represent each place and you would find that there's not much space left. But the producers who actually choose the locations follow certain basic rules. First of all we never (with exceptions in Northern Ireland) visit a place twice. Then we must distribute our visits equally over all parts of the country, and ensure that we have the right proportion of big and small towns, villages and industrial, residential or agricultural districts.

Luckily our files are still full of invitations from people asking us to visit them. So once the area is decided, reference to a file usually produces a place within it where we have been asked to go. There are by now very few big towns unvisited by *DYW*. Since 1972 the only really large place I have been to is Blackburn with just over 100,000 inhabitants, and I think the next largest is Harpenden with about 30,000. Our present average is something between 2,000 to 5,000. Sadly, since I took over we have only been to Northern Ireland three times, though since 1947 there have been thirty-nine visits altogether. But with a non-controversial programme like ours it is practically impossible to talk to people about their town or village and ignore all the terrible things that are going on around them. It would put me in the position of being completely insensitive, and out of touch with their real problems, and to appear to be asking inane and pointless questions.

DYW at one time went abroad mostly to Europe, often to fit in with a Trade Fair or an event like the Olympic Games. But now, except for a short cruise on the S.S. *Canberra* in 1976, we stay at home, though we are hoping to go abroad again. In addition to geographical locations (as they say in *Twenty Questions*) there have been a number of 'one-offs' such as exhibitions, institutions, hospitals, theatres, schools, charities, museums, the three Services, stations, airports, zoos and even an oil rig.

Most of what success *DYW* has depends on the selection of the right six people and this is entirely the responsibility of the producer. There are certain obvious ingredients needed to achieve a properly balanced programme – i.e. one person who can tell the listener as much as possible about a place in as entertaining a way as possible. There must be someone to talk about past events and the history of the place. If it is an industrial town then we probably look for someone from one of the factories, or if it is agricultural then a farmer or a shepherd or someone connected with the countryside. Many places have some sort of traditional ceremony, such as an annual traction-engine fair or a pancake race, and a person is needed to explain these. There is the social side of a town with its clubs, institutions, sports complex, and also the 'do-good' side of a community which is so essential to the happiness of a place. But more important perhaps than any of these, the producer is always on the look-out for a 'character', or the man or woman with an unusual job or hobby. If they have the local dialect and accent so much the better.

We are very conscious of the fact that the majority of the people we interview are on the elderly side. This is inevitable as in general they know far more about a place and its customs, simply because they have lived there longer. 'Characters' too develop the older they grow. So whenever possible we do try to include at least one young person to represent the youthful side of a place – this also helps to liven up the choice of music! There is also the need to get as fair a balance as possible between the sexes, though in spite of Women's Lib I would say we still average four men to two women per programme – it just seems to work out that way.

One of the producer's difficulties is to avoid any similarity with the programmes which have gone out in the previous few weeks. For instance, however old or beautiful a church may be, vicars have to be rationed out, so do farmers, good ladies who run Women's Institutes, Old People's Homes or Meals on Wheels. Everyone naturally wants to mention *everything* which goes on in their town and naturally feels that theirs is better than anyone else's. Quite often we get somebody writing in after a programme asking why we did not include old so and so who is a real character and known to everyone as Mr Whatever the name of the place is. What they don't realise is that the producer has probably visited the person but found that he or she is stone deaf, has a slight stammer or even that we interviewed someone in the same trade or profession only the week before. They may even have refused to take part though this very rarely happens, and when it does it is usually because of excessive modesty or shyness.

How then does the producer make his or her choice? After selecting the place we are to visit something like two or three months in advance, a letter is written to the local town clerk (or his equivalent in these complicated days of council re-organisation) saying that we would like to visit the town and asking the clerk to prepare a list of likely people to interview who can best put the town on the map. Any list they send is of great help but the producers will also have read every guide book available about the place to find out about its industries, history and customs. This will give them a clue as to the type of people they must look for on arrival, when they will not only call on the town clerk, but meet the local press and pick up valuable information in the pubs – often the best sources of all. The producer is also often helped by the original letter suggesting our visit which may include some possible names.

The way we record the programme has changed since it has been produced from Bristol. When it was centred in

London Phyllis Robinson or Richard Burwood used to leave on Sunday night and spend Monday and two-thirds of Tuesday in research and selection. The engineer and I joined them at tea-time on the Tuesday, in time for me to have a quick look-round armed with my guide book which is always sent to me beforehand. After a short briefing about the place and the people selected, we would then do one or possibly two interviews that evening. On Wednesday we would do the remaining four plus my 'top' and 'tail' – or introduction and close, usually finishing mid-afternoon.

To be courteous and polite we have always allowed up to one hour for each person so that we don't appear to rush in and out. This still applies today and Tony Smith and I purposely don't look at our watches until we get up to go and it's amazing how often we find that we have taken between fifty-five and sixty minutes. The producer has of course already met the person to be interviewed, but although he has briefed me beforehand, I always spend the first twenty minutes or so over a cup of tea or coffee getting to know them, finding out about their family and interests – in fact gaining their confidence and making friends. I then know roughly the sort of question I will have to ask to draw them out and get the information which we want in a relaxed way. We then record possibly up to seven minutes depending on the interviewee's ability and clarity in answering my questions. We then have time to play back the interviews so that a husband or wife who has been sent out of the room during the recording can hear the result. We find that most people are far less inhibited if they have no one else in the room except for the producer, the engineer with tape-recorder and myself. Sometimes when a wife is the domineering type, if present she can be tempted to prompt her husband with stage whispers – very offputting! Because some of the people interviewed are busy they can only see us in their factory, office, shop or home at a certain time. So we don't necessarily record the interviews in the exact order in which they will finally go out on the air.

Phyllis Robinson and Richard Burwood used to go back to London and on the Thursday and Friday edit the interviews and time the music before slotting it in between each interview. Every producer makes sure the music *is* available by ringing the Gramophone Library from the location. But if there is any doubt then I put the question about the choice of music *twice*, so that the person interviewed can give an alternative choice.

You may wonder about the editing of the interviews. This is done first of all to 'tidy' up, removing the occasional 'ers' and hesitations, or something which the person regrets having said and would like removed. Or again if the answers given to me are rather monosyllabic it means I have to prompt and encourage the interviewee with a number of supplementary questions. The whole thing then ceases to be a conversation and becomes just a series of questions and answers. But in the editing it is often possible to take out some of my questions so that the answers are joined up to make a more comprehensive reply.

But basically, it's all a matter of the timing and as I've shown, unless the person is outstanding the average interview has to be cut down to just over four minutes. One other thing which has *not* changed is that we choose and interview six people *only* and those are the ones who go out on the air. Some other interview programmes record a number of people and then finally select a few of them. But we don't think that is fair and anyone whom we have interviewed can safely tell his or her friends: 'Listen to me next Sunday at 5.15 pm – I'm on *Down Your Way*.'

But to go back to the way the editing has changed. The programmes from London, once edited on the Friday, used to go out two days later on the Sunday. It is difficult to believe it now but there was *never* a spare programme in reserve in case of an accident to me or the producer or engineer, or even in case the tape got lost or destroyed by mistake. Phyllis backed her luck and with Richard and Jingle only missing one programme each out of more than a thousand and with me luckily fit, she was proved right. But it was a terrific gamble and I often implored her to record at least one in reserve. But she felt that she gained from the topicality and avoided the risk of any of the people interviewed dying if the programme was recorded too far in advance. But of course this policy was the reason for the hurried selection of myself to replace Jingle. He died on the Wednesday night after recording a programme, which with the consent of his widow went out on the following Sunday and Tuesday as usual. But the show had to go on – hence my first *DYW* only six days after Jingle's death.

Partly to avoid this risk but mainly for reasons of time and money there has been a change since we went to Bristol. We now record two programmes in the first week of the month and two in the second, leaving the last fortnight free for editing, in which, by the way, I have no say. I am never present in the studio when it is done. This I think is a good idea as I am too close and involved, whereas the producer has been able to listen to and judge each interview impartially as it's being done. Each pair of programmes are recorded within an area of about sixty square miles to save mileage and time, but they are not put out on the air in successive weeks. For instance, if we record a pair in Oxfordshire and Northants, two programmes, say from Scotland and Wales, would be put on between them. Our recording timetable has also been altered. Tony Smith (or the producer who deputises for him about twelve times a year) now leaves Bristol on a Monday, vets one town from Monday evening to Tuesday evening and then travels the sixty miles or so to the next place. By the time the engineer and myself have arrived on Wednesday evening he has made his selections. We sometimes do one interview that night and five the next day before setting off for the first town which Tony vetted on the Tuesday. We finish sometime on Friday afternoon ready for a nice peaceful weekend.

It's a tightly-timed but well-organised timetable and we still find that each place takes around six hours to do, though the kind hospitality of people does sometimes mean that we get behind the clock. It's not unusual to be offered tea or coffee, biscuits and home-made cakes at all four houses or offices which we visit in a morning. We have learnt to say 'no thank you' politely but sometimes when the tray is laid out ready we don't have the heart to do so, no matter how much our stomachs complain. We appreciate that although it's just another pleasant day's work for us, *DYW* only visits a place once in a lifetime, so in a small way it's quite a big day for the 'victim'. Luckily I have never had the same experience as Richard Dimbleby who once had to squeeze in three interviews in one evening. As a result in each house he visited the table was laid either for high tea or supper and he bravely did justice to all three! But he did have more room for it than me!

It's the same everywhere we go. We invariably get a very warm welcome and this really does make my job rewarding. I was, however, once slightly surprised by a greeting from an effusive and friendly lady. She flung open her front door and said: 'Oh, Mr Johnston, how nice to see you. I have always wanted to meet you. And do tell me – how big is your apparatus?!!' I can only think that she was referring to our engineer's equipment – if you see what I mean!

As you can imagine, *DYW* involves a lot of travelling and I usually go by car except to Scotland when I either fly or use the train. Trains have a funny effect on me. I hope I am a fairly gregarious and friendly person but once inside a railway carriage I shut up like a clam. Even if there's only one other person I never say a word but just slump behind my newspaper. It sounds dreadfully unfriendly but I find there are quite a few people who do the same. At any rate the late Lord Justice Birkett – the best after-dinner speaker I have ever heard – once told a lovely story which bears it out.

He was speaking at the 1953 Cricket Writers' Dinner to Lindsay Hassett's Australian Touring Team. He said how delighted everyone was to see them and told them what a great welcome they would get wherever they went all over the country. But he did give a slight warning. 'Don't be put off,' he said, 'by the apparent aloofness and reserve of the British people. We are not really cold and unfriendly but just hide our feelings. Indeed, we treat each other in exactly the same way, so there is no need for you to worry.'

Lord Birkett then went on to tell the following story to prove his point. One day as the Flying Scotsman left King's Cross on its non-stop journey to Edinburgh there were four people sitting in one carriage, each in a corner seat reading his newspaper. There was complete silence, except for the slight rustle of paper, as the train glided swiftly through the Hertfordshire countryside. After it had passed through

Hitchin about thirty-two miles out of London, one of the men could bear it no longer. He put down his *Times* and said: 'Look, this is ridiculous. We are going to be alone in this carriage non-stop for four hundred miles. Let's get to know each other and have a chat. This silence is unbearable. I'll start off by telling you something about myself. I'm a Brigadier. I'm married and I have one son who is a solicitor.'

The man sitting opposite him put down *his Times* and said: 'This is an amazing coincidence. *I'm* also a Brigadier. I'm married and I also have one son who is a banker.'

The third man then put down his *Times* and he said: 'This is ridiculous. You'll never believe this. I'm also a Brigadier. I'm also married and have one son who is a schoolmaster.' All three of them looked at the fourth man who was still sitting quietly behind his *Daily Mirror*. 'Come on,' they said to him, 'join in and tell us something about yourself.' A gruff voice from behind the paper said: 'Sorry, I'd rather not,' and then silence reigned again. So the other three ignored him and chatted among themselves for about half an hour and then decided to try again. 'Come on,' they said, 'be a sport, do join in.' 'Oh well, have it your own way,' said the man as he reluctantly put down the *Daily Mirror*. '*I* am a Regimental Sergeant Major. I am NOT married. I have three sons – and they are, all three, Brigadiers!'

While on the subject of trains there was the bishop who was sitting in the corner seat of a crowded carriage doing *The Times* crossword puzzle. He seemed to be getting on pretty well and filling in a lot of the answers. But he began to look puzzled and putting down his paper asked the other passengers: 'Could any of you kindly help me? I want a four-letter word with female affiliations ending in UNT.' There was a slight pause and then a young man suggested: 'What about AUNT, sir?' 'Ah,' said the bishop with relief, 'that's it. I thought I must be wrong. Have any of you got a rubber?'

But, as usual, I have digressed, and now a final word about *Down Your Way*. It is a wonderful programme to do and as with so much of my life I have been unbelievably lucky to get the job. We are unashamedly square and uncontroversial. We go to a place to find out the good things about it, and never look 'under the carpet' for the sort of things which hit

the headlines in the popular press. We just try to find nice people who will reflect all these good things. It is one of the satisfying features of *DYW* that there *are* so many nice people about. We are told *ad nauseam* of the terrible things which go on in our society and how mean and self-centred people are. Up to a point this is obviously true. On the other hand you come round the country with me and it really will cheer you up to meet so many people who are devoting so much of their lives or leisure time to helping others. Call them do-gooders – or what you like. But their numbers are legion and they are the salt of the earth. I like to think that they are the true heart of Britain. It all sounds terribly old-fashioned and patriotic – but I *do* mean it. In addition of course I learn a little about a lot, and discover old buildings, customs and traditions which have been in existence for centuries. There's also the joy of journeying all over Britain which in spite of the growth of towns and the spreading tentacles of industry still remains to me the most beautiful country in the world.

The most important part of *Down Your Way* to me is th
memory of the people whom I have interviewed. By no
they number fifteen hundred, so I can obviously only men
tion a fraction of them. I suppose pride of place must go t
the only centurion whom I have so far interviewed in th
programme – Mrs Emma Brewster of Radcliffe on Tren
She was as bright as a cricket and oked wonderfully fit an
alert as she sat in her armchair by the fire. She had good ne
knows how many great-grandchildren and was loving
looked after by one of her granddaughters. During th
interview I asked her whether she had received a telegra
from the Queen on her hundredth birthday. 'Oh, yes,' s
said, 'I did, but I was very disappointed. It wasn't in her o
handwriting. I think she must be getting old and bored w
doing it so often. I know I would be!'

Then there was the vegetarian from Usk in Wales w
during the war was sent out to India to run the mule tra
port. Knowing he would be short of the green stuff out th
he took with him a lot of mustard and cress seeds. Each ni
at the end of a hot sticky day he would take off his welling
boots and plant some seeds inside them. By next day he
some fresh(?) mustard and cress to eat with his curry
lunch.

Talking of wellies – when we went to Presteigne in Po
a young farmer called John Davies, who was a cham
sheep shearer, told us about an unusual competitive s
which was very popular in those parts. It was w
wanging, and it used to take place at all the local fairs
fêtes. It is very similar to throwing the javelin except that
hurl a wellington boot instead. The good throwers get qu

the headlines in the popular press. We just try to find nice people who will reflect all these good things. It is one of the satisfying features of *DYW* that there *are* so many nice people about. We are told *ad nauseam* of the terrible things which go on in our society and how mean and self-centred people are. Up to a point this is obviously true. On the other hand you come round the country with me and it really will cheer you up to meet so many people who are devoting so much of their lives or leisure time to helping others. Call them do-gooders – or what you like. But their numbers are legion and they are the salt of the earth. I like to think that they are the true heart of Britain. It all sounds terribly old-fashioned and patriotic – but I *do* mean it. In addition of course I learn a little about a lot, and discover old buildings, customs and traditions which have been in existence for centuries. There's also the joy of journeying all over Britain which in spite of the growth of towns and the spreading tentacles of industry still remains to me the most beautiful country in the world.

Fourth Over Nice people

The most important part of *Down Your Way* to me is the memory of the people whom I have interviewed. By now they number fifteen hundred, so I can obviously only mention a fraction of them. I suppose pride of place must go to the only centurion whom I have so far interviewed in the programme – Mrs Emma Brewster of Radcliffe on Trent. She was as bright as a cricket and looked wonderfully fit and alert as she sat in her armchair by the fire. She had goodness knows how many great-grandchildren and was lovingly looked after by one of her granddaughters. During the interview I asked her whether she had received a telegram from the Queen on her hundredth birthday. 'Oh, yes,' she said, 'I did, but I was very disappointed. It wasn't in her own handwriting. I think she must be getting old and bored with doing it so often. I know I would be!'

Then there was the vegetarian from Usk in Wales who during the war was sent out to India to run the mule transport. Knowing he would be short of the green stuff out there he took with him a lot of mustard and cress seeds. Each night at the end of a hot sticky day he would take off his wellington boots and plant some seeds inside them. By next day he had some fresh(?) mustard and cress to eat with his curry for lunch.

Talking of wellies – when we went to Presteigne in Powys a young farmer called John Davies, who was a champion sheep shearer, told us about an unusual competitive sport which was very popular in those parts. It was welly-wanging, and it used to take place at all the local fairs and fêtes. It is very similar to throwing the javelin except that you hurl a wellington boot instead. The good throwers get quite a

the headlines in the popular press. We just try to find nice people who will reflect all these good things. It is one of the satisfying features of *DYW* that there *are* so many nice people about. We are told *ad nauseam* of the terrible things which go on in our society and how mean and self-centred people are. Up to a point this is obviously true. On the other hand you come round the country with me and it really will cheer you up to meet so many people who are devoting so much of their lives or leisure time to helping others. Call them do-gooders – or what you like. But their numbers are legion and they are the salt of the earth. I like to think that they are the true heart of Britain. It all sounds terribly old-fashioned and patriotic – but I *do* mean it. In addition of course I learn a little about a lot, and discover old buildings, customs and traditions which have been in existence for centuries. There's also the joy of journeying all over Britain which in spite of the growth of towns and the spreading tentacles of industry still remains to me the most beautiful country in the world.

Fourth Over Nice people

The most important part of *Down Your Way* to me is the memory of the people whom I have interviewed. By now they number fifteen hundred, so I can obviously only mention a fraction of them. I suppose pride of place must go to the only centurion whom I have so far interviewed in the programme – Mrs Emma Brewster of Radcliffe on Trent. She was as bright as a cricket and looked wonderfully fit and alert as she sat in her armchair by the fire. She had goodness knows how many great-grandchildren and was lovingly looked after by one of her granddaughters. During the interview I asked her whether she had received a telegram from the Queen on her hundredth birthday. 'Oh, yes,' she said, 'I did, but I was very disappointed. It wasn't in her own handwriting. I think she must be getting old and bored with doing it so often. I know I would be!'

Then there was the vegetarian from Usk in Wales who during the war was sent out to India to run the mule transport. Knowing he would be short of the green stuff out there he took with him a lot of mustard and cress seeds. Each night at the end of a hot sticky day he would take off his wellington boots and plant some seeds inside them. By next day he had some fresh(?) mustard and cress to eat with his curry for lunch.

Talking of wellies – when we went to Presteigne in Powys a young farmer called John Davies, who was a champion sheep shearer, told us about an unusual competitive sport which was very popular in those parts. It was welly-wanging, and it used to take place at all the local fairs and fêtes. It is very similar to throwing the javelin except that you hurl a wellington boot instead. The good throwers get quite a good distance – something in the region of forty yards. John told us with delight that the ladies also ran a competition and that the local lady welly-wanging champion was a Mrs Woolley from Willey!

There was a lovely old lady of well over eighty in the small town of Penkridge in Staffordshire. She was a farmer's daughter and still delivered milk round the town each day. She lived in her father's old house where she had been born. It had been a farm but was now a terraced house in a street. The remarkable thing she told us was that in all her life she had never spent *a single night away from the house*. She had been to London for the day and on several coach trips to the seaside, but had always returned at night to sleep in her own house. The only concession she made in this extraordinary tale was that she had not always slept in the same room. I found it very difficult to take in when I thought of the many hundreds of nights I myself have spent away from home either on my job or on holiday.

When in Buckfastleigh for *Down Your Way* I was told the following story of a new vicar at the parish church on the top of the hill above the town. He was being taken round the churchyard by the verger who was giving him a potted history of the various people buried there. When they came to one tombstone the verger said: 'This was Harry – I warned him but he wouldn't listen. I told him that the cider would be the death of him and would get him in the end. And it did. He went on drinking it in spite of all my warnings.' The vicar stooped down to read the writing on the tombstone, and read: 'Harry——, who died aged 96 years on——.'

In St Davids Dyfed – the smallest cathedral city – we came across the local baker, a great talker and character called Dai Evans. He kept a donkey which drank beer and was famous for miles around for his homemade bread and cakes. Inevitably he was called Dai The Crust. His greatest triumph was on a visit to the district by Prince Charles. Dai had the honour to present one of his special loaves personally to the Prince of Wales. From then on he assumed the title of Dai the *Upper* Crust!

Anthony Beard was a young farmer at Widecombe-in-the Moor in Devon, of Uncle Tom Cobley fame. He did a milk round in the local villages, and incidentally used plastic instead of glass milk bottles and so saved himself the time and labour of having to collect and wash them. In his spare time he was an entertainer singing West Country songs and telling stories in the Devonshire dialect. He even yodelled and composed his own songs. One of the stories was about a farmer who often milked the cows in the open fields to save bringing them back to the farm. One summer evening he was milking away when a holidaymaker leant over the hedge and asked him if he knew the time. The farmer put his hand under the cow's udder and replied: 'Ten minutes to six, mister,' and went on with his milking.

The holidaymaker was amazed and rushed off back to the village to fetch his wife to see this extraordinary countryman who could tell the time by putting his hand under a cow's udder. The couple came back in about twenty minutes and found the farmer milking another cow at the same spot by the hedge. The holidaymaker persuaded his wife to ask the time. Once again the farmer put his hand under the cow's udder and replied: 'Just on ten minutes past six.' The couple thanked him and went off dumbfounded at what they had seen. In explanation Anthony added: 'What the farmer didn't tell them was that each time he lifted the cow's udder, he could see the clock on the church tower.'

When we visited North Berwick – that mecca of golfing – Mrs Doreen Stevenson told us about the old professional, Ben Sayers, renowned maker of golf clubs and with a great reputation as a teacher. At one time North Berwick was very fashionable with politicians who came there to breathe the invigorating air and of course to play golf. Lord Balfour and Sir John Simon were frequent visitors and one day Ben was partnering Lord Balfour in a foursome. They were playing on the No. 1 links which runs along by the sea and on which in the old days the local farmers had grazing rights.

At one hole Lord Balfour drove off and his ball went straight down the middle but landed slap in the middle of a juicy cow pat. Lord Balfour thought this was very funny and laughingly apologised to Ben, but said it was his shot and that he would have to 'get out of the mess'. But the wily Ben took a mashie and after taking deliberate aim played a complete air shot. 'I'm sorry, m'lord,' he said with a cunning smile, 'I'm afraid I got a fly in my eye, which made me miss it completely. Now it's *your* turn to get it out!'

One of the most cheerful people I have ever met in *DYW* was Syd Hart who had spent most of his life in the Cheshire Home at Ampthill suffering from multiple-sclerosis. In spite of all his trouble life seemed to be one big joke to him, and he apologised during our interview for not speaking too clearly. He explained that in his hurry to get ready he had put in someone else's false teeth by mistake!

Then there was Arthur Roland of the little village of Alston in Cumbria. He kept – of all things – a bottle shop. Just rows and rows of empty bottles – eight thousand of them, of all shapes, sizes and colours. Some were worth twenty pounds or more and people from all over the world descend on Arthur to add to their own collections. The surprising thing about Arthur was that he did not drink anything except tea.

In Ruthin, North Wales, we discovered a young girl called Patricia Evers-Swindell who remarkably painted on *cobwebs*. She lived in an old house with some old stables attached. She collected the cobwebs from these, some still with the spider and dead flies in them. She then covered them thinly with milk to take some of the stickiness out of them and then painted on them with ordinary brush and paint. Dogs' heads were her speciality and by framing the web between two pieces of glass she obtained an excellent three-dimensional effect.

The great thing about doing *DYW* is that we are always learning something new. I personally had never heard of a Foaling Bank but we came across one in Newport, Shropshire. It had been started by Joanna Vardon as a completely new idea, and was the only one in the world. It was really a sort of swap shop. All over the country a number of mares die giving birth to their foals and so leave orphans to be looked after. Alternatively a number of foals die at birth or are stillborn, leaving an unhappy mother with lots of milk and no foal to drink it.

So Joanna Vardon had what was really a very simple idea,

but a very difficult and complicated one to carry out. She thought what a waste it was of foal-less mares and mother-less foals. So why not bring the two together? This she has done in a remarkable way and people from all over the country – and even from abroad – arrive at all times of the day or night with horse-boxes – or even a mini in the case of one tiny foal lying on the back seat! Speed is the essence of the operation as a mare's milk dries up in about twenty-four hours if there is no foal to suckle her. There is also the problem of a mare accepting a foal which is not her own. Joanna found that she had to skin the dead foal and wrap its skin round the orphan foal before the mare would accept it. A rather gruesome business but carried out cheerfully by Joanna Vardon and her band of lady helpers. It should also be pointed out that the whole scheme is non-profit making and people pay what they can afford. Since the bank started in 1966 Joanna and her staff have dealt with well over five thousand cases.

At Budleigh Salterton we had the pleasure of meeting 'Golden Voice' – alias Stuart Hibberd, the first ever BBC radio announcer. Now aged eighty-four he was amazingly hale and hearty and entertained us before the interview with songs and recitations without any music or notes. He re-called the early days at Savoy Hill when all the announcers had to change into dinner jackets at 6 pm. At first he wore a stiff shirt but the engineers complained that it made crack-ling noises into the microphone, so from then on he had to wear a soft one.

He denied making some of the well-known gaffes which are generally attributed to him, such as:

'There'll now be an interlush by Ernest Lude';

'We are now going over to the bathroom at Pump';

'You will now hear the bum of the flightelbee.'

But he *did* admit to two. During a weather forecast he once said that there would be 'heal and slate' instead of 'sleet and hail'. And when introducing a programme of American music he announced that the next piece would be *The Star Bangled Spanner*!

He made one amusing slip during our interview. I said that I understood that he still played a part in the life of the church at Budleigh. 'Yes,' he said, 'I still read the news – hmm lesson, every Sunday evening.'

At Goring on Thames I interviewed the wartime Commander-in-Chief, Bomber Command, Marshal of the Royal Air Force, Sir Arthur Harris, nicknamed Bomber. I was a bit apprehensive as I had never met him before and outwardly he had always seemed to be a tough stand-no-nonsense sort of character. He had certainly had to fight hard throughout the war on behalf of his Bomber Command, and had a reputation of speaking his mind, with no fear of anyone. Anyway, we thought we must make sure to be punctual for our interview and so get off to a good start.

As a result, we were in fact a few minutes in advance of the time arranged. After we had rung the bell of his charming riverside house, the well-known figure opened the door and in a gruff voice barked out: 'You're early,' in such a way that it appeared to be a bigger crime than being late. However he soon smiled and welcomed us and we spent a delightful hour with him in his study. There were pictures of all types of aeroplanes dating from the early days of the 1914 war and signed photographs of all the great war leaders, from Sir Winston and General Eisenhower downwards. There were letters and memos written on paper with headings of No. 10 Downing Street or SHAPE headquarters.

There were war mementoes everywhere, and the one he said he treasured most was a half-smoked cigar lying proudly in a glass case. He had attended Sir Winston's farewell dinner as Prime Minister which he gave at Chequers in 1953. Sir Winston had insisted that he smoke one of his famous torpedo-size cigars. Unfortunately, Sir Arthur was a non-smoker and admitted that after a few puffs he had had to leave the room in a hurry! But he kept the cigar and it was obvious that he worshipped Sir Winston and was grateful for all the support and help he had received from him.

Many people – MPs and other commanders in the services especially – were constantly sniping at Sir Arthur and making life difficult for him. I asked him why Bomber Command never got the full appreciation and recognition which it undoubtedly deserved. He thought that it was because people, having been bombed themselves, disliked bombs.

The public also never saw the direct results of his bomber's work whereas the more glamorous Fighter Command could be seen in action in the skies defending our homes. I also asked him why he was not given a peerage like all the other war leaders. He said that after the war Winston had said he would ask Mr Attlee to give him a peerage but that he, Sir Arthur, had refused and was content to accept a baronetcy in 1953. But he seemed to have no bitterness and to be living a happy and contented life among the friendly people of Goring. He had obviously lost none of his guts and determination because on the day before I saw him he had judged the local Jubilee Baby Competition in the town – and that *does* take courage.

Incidentally, Sir Arthur was not like Monty, who during a battle went to bed as usual at 10 pm and woe betide anyone who disturbed him. Sir Arthur admitted that whenever his bombers were out, except for the odd cat-nap he never went to sleep and was available for instant decisions at any time of the night. He was never made into a war hero like some of the others, but after meeting him I am convinced that Bomber Command and the nation owe him much gratitude and possibly a slight apology for the somewhat churlish way he was treated.

At Coldstream in Berwickshire I interviewed Henry Douglas-Home, brother of Lord Home and a well-known ornithologist and broadcaster in Scotland. In fact he is known up there as the Birdman and I talked to him in a glade of a wood on the Hirsel Estate – family home of the Homes. It was from here that he used to compete with *his* birds against me with *my* birds from a wood at Hever in Kent. These friendly competitions were great fun to do and were done 'live'. We both had microphones placed strategically throughout our woods to catch the song of as many birds as possible. Percy Edwards was the judge and noted down all the different birds he heard, each side taking it in turns to broadcast, and the one with the most species of birds heard was the winner. The results were always very close, though on one occasion Henry did accuse me of cheating! I must say I was once very suspicious of him too when, with the scores level, we suddenly heard a cuckoo from his wood – a most unlikely bird to hear at the time of the year when we were broadcasting. There is in fact the hoot of an owl in the archives in Scotland which Henry recorded, saying it was the most perfect reproduction he had ever heard. It was only years later that his brother William admitted that it had been him hooting behind a bush! No wonder I was suspicious about that cuckoo!

Henry told us two delightful stories about the Home family. On one occasion he and his two brothers, Alec and William, were turning out things in the Hirsel cellars when they came upon a large stuffed crocodile with wicked gleaming eyes. Their Aunt Olive was coming to lunch so they thought that they would play a trick on her. William took the crocodile and placed it on a rock in one of the streams running through the Hirsel grounds. After lunch he took his aunt for a walk, and led her to a bridge crossing the stream. Suddenly William gave a shout and pointed: 'Look, Aunt Olive, quick, we'd better run. There's a crocodile down there on the rock.' But instead of screaming or running for her life, Aunt Olive kept completely calm. 'Really,' she said, 'I didn't know that they came this far north!' But was she pulling William's leg or did she mean what she said?

The Homes had a wonderful Jeeves-like butler called Collingwood, and one day before the war someone said to the old Lord Home: 'I'm sorry to tell you, m'lord, but I think Collingwood is going mad. Early this morning at 7 am I saw him walking over a ploughed field in full butler's rig. Black coat, striped trousers and all, talking and singing to himself.' On investigation Lord Home discovered what had happened. His youngest son, George, was a very keen birdwatcher and used to go off at 5.30 am to a hide to watch the birds through binoculars. But he found that the birds, having seen him arrive, were aware of his presence, and stayed quietly out of sight. So George persuaded Collingwood to go with him one morning, much against Collingwood's will. He finally agreed but said he would have to come fully dressed as he had to be back in time to take up early morning tea to Lord and Lady Home. The idea was that the birds would see George and Collingwood go together into the hide, and that after a short time Collingwood would ostentatiously leave it, singing and talking to himself to attract the attention of the birds. The hope was that the birds would be fooled into thinking that the 'enemy' had now gone, not noticing that although two had arrived only one had left. Anyhow, that was the explanation of the singing butler.

One of the most unusual and eccentric people I have ever interviewed was Richard Booth of Hay-on-Wye. He was unusual because he has turned Hay into a book town. He has six second-hand book shops with over two million books on about fifteen miles of shelving. His object is to have as many books as possible on each subject, so that someone who is, say, interested in bridge or gardening can go to Hay and be directed to shelf after shelf on his or her subject. In no other bookshop in the world would it be possible to find such a concentration of books on so many different subjects. Visitors come to Hay from all over the world and there is an annual book week with lots of celebrations.

Richard buys his books in vast quantities, and when I went to see him he was just back from America where he had bought up a hundred thousand second-hand books. Just think of the job of sorting that lot, and then the even more difficult task of deciding on the right price for each one after buying them in bulk. He admitted that he must sometimes unknowingly buy up a rare first edition and let it slip through his fingers.

He was eccentric because on 1 April 1977 he declared Hay-on-Wye independent and indeed I received an invitation to the opening ceremony. He was also in the process of appointing his own ambassadors to various countries.

It was as you can imagine a fascinating interview to do and it had a most surprising and hilarious ending which alas the listeners never heard. When I asked Richard for his choice of music I caught his eye and for some unknown reason he got the giggles – or in theatrical language he 'corpsed'. So did we all, but luckily the engineer kept recording and I often play the tape when I want a good laugh. It's quite hysterical. He was laughing so much that to start with he couldn't get a word out. So I kept on repeating my question in between my own laughs. Gradually through his chokes and sobs he managed to blurt out that he wanted *Golden Years* or anything by David Bowie.

I must have asked him at least ten times for his music before his answer was considered good enough to go in the programme. Although they did not hear the laughing tape on *Down Your Way* listeners did hear it at the end of a programme I did with producer Michael Craig called *It's A Funny Business*. I explained what had happened and then we just played the hoots of laughter. Jimmy Tarbuck told me sometime afterwards that he was motoring along listening to the programme, and began to laugh so much that he had to pull into the side of the road until it had finished.

And then there was a young chap called Chris Fleming at Wem in Shropshire. He played a big part in organising activities in the town and also ran a disco. He advertised it as 'the most boring disco in the world', chiefly because his Shropshire customers demanded a squarer type of music than is normally played in discos. He wore an earring on his left ear. I asked him why only *one* earring and not one on his right ear. 'Well,' he replied, 'I would look an awful fool if I wore two, wouldn't I?'

Jack Pharoah of Ravenglass was an amusing character and one of those people who seem to be able to turn their hands to anything. When I interviewed him he had a cobbler's shop and kept a garage. But he had been a fisherman, a ferryman and a guide to the local bird sanctuary, among other things. He was not above a bit of subterfuge to help to boost trade. As a ferryman he used to ferry visitors across to the sanctuary. But at low tides it was just possible for them to walk across if they so wished. So to discourage them he used to get his son to walk across the sands in full view of the visitors. Then suddenly his son would pretend to be sinking into the sand and mud, as if caught in some quicksand. Naturally enough after that, most visitors opted to go across by boat!

Jack also once worked quite a clever trick on the owner of a Rolls-Royce. The man drove up in his Rolls and asked Jack to fill it up, while he went across the road to get some cigarettes. He was in such a hurry that he left the engine of the Rolls running. When he got back he asked Jack how many gallons he had put in. 'Seventeen, sir,' said Jack 'But,' protested the Rolls' owner, 'the car only holds fifteen gallons.' 'I know,' said Jack, thinking quickly, 'but as you left the engine running it used two gallons while I was filling the car up!'

We received a double bonus when we visited Harpenden in the shape of Lord Hill and Eric Morecambe. Lord Hill, Cabinet Minister and, uniquely, chairman, in succession, of both ITA and BBC, is still best known to many people as the war-time Radio Doctor. He told me how he was the first man ever to mention the word 'bowels' on the air with that deep bedside voice of his. His philosophy in his radio talks was to give confidence to his listeners and discourage them from worrying about their health. 'Leave it alone. It won't get better if you pick it,' was a typical bit of advice.

As for Eric, what a lovely person he is. Modest, kind, friendly, a great worker for charity but perhaps most important of all, a naturally funny man. He doesn't have to try to be funny. He just is. Jokes come automatically to him no matter to whom he is talking. During our interview, which was completely unrehearsed, I asked him why he came to live in Harpenden. 'Oh, we came here one day to sell my mother-in-law . . .', or again when I asked him about the running 'feud' between him and Des O'Connor, 'Oh, we're great friends really. He even came to my daughter's wedding – he wasn't asked, but he came.' Eric is a keen ornithologist, so I asked him if he went out walking with big binoculars. 'Oh, no,' he said, 'I leave Big Binoculars behind. He's not too keen on birds.' And so on.

Eric is a most rewarding person to talk to, and genuinely fond of Harpenden and its inhabitants. They all know him by sight of course and he enjoys going shopping and talking to them. 'It's only when I go to Luton that I put on dark glasses and a limp . . .'

One of the joys of doing *Down Your Way* is the chats we have with people both before and especially after the interview. Afterwards they are always relaxed and come up with some splendid gossip and stories about their town or village. In one Yorkshire town which we visited one of our 'victims' told us about a local lady who was well known for never giving anything to charity if she could help it. However hard people tried to persuade her she used to invent all sorts of excuses, one of her favourites being that she was deaf and couldn't hear what was being said. Not knowing this, one evening a man walked up her drive and rang her front doorbell. After some delay she came to the door and asked him what he wanted.

'Well, madam,' he said, 'I apologise for troubling you but I wonder if you would be generous and help a good cause. I am collecting on behalf of the Brighouse and Rastrick Band Instrumental Purchase and Repair Fund.' 'It's no good,' she said with her voice raised, 'I can't hear a word you are saying. Please shout it louder.' So the man repeated his request at the top of his voice. But it was still no good, and the lady shook her head, cupping her hand behind her ear.

Once again the man tried, as loud and as deliberately as possible. But the lady said, 'It's no good. I still can't hear a word. You'll have to go away.' The man looked very disappointed and muttered quietly under his breath: 'Stuff her, the stingy old bitch' – at which the lady said: 'Yes, and you too can stuff your Brighouse and Rastrick Brass Band Instrumental Purchase and Repair Fund' – and slammed the door in his face.

Inevitably, as I've said, we tend to talk to a good many elderly people, and a friendly colleague warned me of one pitfall into which he had fallen. He was interviewing a very old lady who was ill in bed. Sitting by her bedside he asked her. 'Have you ever been bed-ridden before?' 'Yes, young man,' she replied, 'I have many times. And I've got ten children to prove it!' So that is *one* question I never ask!

And another warning to would-be interviewers. Never judge people's age by their appearance, as a mythical broadcaster is 'reputed' to have discovered to his cost! He was visiting an old people's home to find out why some people live to such a ripe old age. He picked out the three oldest men he could see, and asked each one the same questions. How old are you, and to what do you attribute your old age?

The first old man said he was a hundred and two and had never smoked in his life, had always gone to bed at ten o'clock every night and had been happily married for sixty-five years.

The second said he was a hundred and six, had never

drunk, took a long walk every day and although a bachelor had enjoyed a healthy sex life as a young man.

The third old man looked particularly frail and wizened. He said he had never gone to bed before 2 am, drank at least two bottles of whisky and smoked sixty cigarettes a day. But most important of all he had enjoyed sex at least three times every night with any woman he could find.

The interviewer was flabbergasted as he gazed at the wrinkled old face ravaged by time. 'Well,' he said, 'I don't know how you've done it. Remarkable. But I don't think you said how old you are.' 'Twenty-eight next birthday,' replied the 'old' man.

All this travelling round the country staying in different hotels can have its complications – as my friend Henry Blofeld, the cricket writer and commentator, once found to his cost. He was reporting a county match at Nottingham and for the first night stayed at the Bridgford Hotel. But because they were booked up he had to move to the Albany Hotel for the next two nights. He had a good dinner with a few aperitifs and a bottle of wine and then went up to his room for an early night feeling 'nicely thank you'.

As he always does he slept in the nude, and woke at about 2 am wanting to spend a penny. So in a sleepy, bemused state he got out of bed, groped his way round the room and found a door which he thought was the bathroom. He went through it and it shut with a click behind him. He then looked for the loo but to his horror found he was standing in the brightly-lit corridor outside his room, without a stitch of clothing on and without his key. He was by now wide awake and quickly spotted a tray on the floor outside the next-door room. He whipped the paper napkin from under the plates and held it in front of his vital parts.

He realised that he must get hold of the night porter to open his door for him with a pass key. So he crept along the deserted corridor to the lift, which to his relief started coming up when he pressed the button. When it arrived he got in and pressed 'Ground Floor', intending when he reached there to call out to the night porter for help. The lift began to descend but to his alarm he felt it slowing up as it approached the second floor. Someone had obviously pushed the button and sure enough as the lift stopped at the gates there waiting to get in was a party of men and women in evening dress, laughing and joking after what had obviously been a very good evening.

The laughter stopped for a second as they saw Henry crouching at the back of the lift desperately clutching the inadequate napkin against himself. Then of course there was uproar, with roars of laughter, and a few shrill squeaks from the ladies. Luckily they had not opened the gates so Henry quickly pushed the ground-floor button again and the lift shot down out of sight of the party. He explained what had happened to a surprised night porter, not used to seeing naked men approaching his desk in the middle of the night. He gave Henry a pass key and saw him into the lift, which luckily raced up past the party on the second floor still recovering from shock. So Henry slunk back to his room and ever since has made sure that he knows the geography of every hotel room before he goes to sleep. A lesson for us all!

Luckily I don't often have to travel by tube – at least during the rush hour. Unlike a friend of mine who had to travel to and from the City every day. He was once standing in a crowded carriage with bodies pressed closely together. He suddenly realised to his embarrassment that he had left his trousers unzipped and was in danger of exposing himself. So, hoping no one would notice, he surreptitiously managed to get his hand down and slowly pull up his zip. He then relaxed and looked about him pretending that nothing had happened.

When the train stopped at the next station (which was not the one he wanted) he found himself being drawn mysteriously towards the sliding doors, following very closely behind a very attractive blonde. He tried to stop but was dragged on to the platform and as she made her way to the exit, he realised that he was attached in some way. He desperately tried to explain to her as she snapped at him to leave her alone and stop following her. Finally she tried to turn round but found that she could not do so. They then both found out what had happened. His zip had got caught in the back of her fur coat and a lot of fiddling had to go on before he could free himself by undoing the zip. Quite a crowd had gathered round them, as he apologised profusely to the blonde, who in the end saw the joke. But as he did himself up blushing like mad, my friend there and then decided to have fly buttons on his next pair of trousers.

Whether out of kindness or not I don't know, but within a few days of learning that *Down Your Way* was coming off, I was asked to become a member of a new *Twenty Questions* team. This, too, caused quite a furore as except for Anona Winn all the members of the old panel were to be discarded. It seemed bad luck on them, especially Joy Adamson who had been on the panel for twenty-five years and Norman Hackforth who for eighteen years had been either the mystery voice or one of the panel. The new question-master in place of Peter Jones was to be Terry Wogan, and in addition to Anona and myself our panel was completed by humourist William Rushton and a charming actress Bettine Le Beau.

But of course as a professional broadcaster one must accept any opportunity which is offered, without allowing one's feelings to interfere, and I'm sure the old panel understood this. Anyway, we were on a hiding to nothing because in fact *Twenty Questions* is not an easy game to play. In order not to waste questions team spirit is essential and this can only develop after several series together. There is the knack of knowing the right questions to ask early on to establish in which area the object is. For instance, if it is Animal someone must ask: 'Is it human?' If so, then: 'Alive or dead? Fact or fiction? Are there lots of them? Only one,' etc.

If it is *not* human then: 'How many legs? Domestic or wild? Do you eat it? Is it something made from an animal?' For Vegetable you obviously start with: 'Can you eat it? Is it a growing plant? Can you wear it? Is it wooden, rubber etc?' And for Mineral you have to establish whether it is wet or dry, metal or stone, natural or handmade. That leaves the hardest of them all, Abstract, which can be almost anything and the recognised first question here is: 'With what sense do you recognise it?' After that the best of luck! It's hit or miss.

So you can realise that there is a lot of skill needed which is only acquired by practice and knowing what the other team members are thinking. Plus of course that unbelievable intuition with which Anona Winn seems to be gifted. Willie

Rushton proved to be a splendid guesser, keeping quiet for possibly two-thirds of the questions and then suddenly popping up with the correct answer – which proves the value of listening carefully to the answers given by the question-master. Bettine with her broken accent and innocent charm managed to inveigle far more helpful answers from Terry than any of us.

We did thirteen programmes altogether, recording two in an evening or at lunchtime in front of an invited audience at the old Playhouse Theatre near the Embankment. In case you have never been one of these audiences the procedure is for the mystery voice (tucked away somewhere in the bowels of the theatre) to give the object to the listeners unheard, of course, by the panel. At the same time as he is speaking two brown-coated attendants carry a board across the front of the stage with the object printed on it for the audience to see. But again, of course, the panel are not in the know. It is all absolutely above board and I am convinced that no producer has ever divulged the answers or even given hints to the panel beforehand.

We recorded the programmes throughout the summer and not surprisingly in my opinion we were nowhere near as good as the old panel, which I hope was some small comfort to them! We got a little better the more practice we had, but our producer, Alastair Scott-Johnston, did not make it easy for us. He had a special delight in giving us the dreaded Abstract objects so that our percentage of victories over Terry was not as high as it should have been. Just to show what people thought of us, two old ladies were leaving the Playhouse after two of our recordings. Someone heard one of them ask the other: 'Did you enjoy it dear?' 'Yes, I did,' the other replied, 'very much indeed. But you know I *still* prefer *Twenty Questions*!'

But it was all great fun to do and under Terry's cheerful guidance we were a very happy team. The only thing I did *not* look forward to was the solo spot which really was rather frightening. You are out on your own with no help from the rest of the team. Often your mind goes a complete blank when it is quite obvious to everyone else what the object is. For instance, for one of my solos, the object was Animal or

Vegetable. By the applause and laughter of the audience when they read what the object was, I suspected it would be something personal. After a few questions I established it had to do with cricket but failed to get it in twenty questions. I could have kicked myself afterwards. The answer was – a bat.

Fifth Over All's right with the World Cup

The year 1975 was a great summer for cricket. The sun shone, there was the first ever World Cup Tournament, the Prudential Cup, and the added bonus of a four-match Test series against Australia.

The Prudential Cup was an unqualified success. Eight countries took part and during an unbelievable fortnight of uninterrupted blue sky there were fifteen matches played of one innings each with a maximum of sixty overs. Naturally the two junior members of the International Cricket Conference – Sri Lanka and East Africa – were outclassed, but there was some thrilling cricket watched by large crowds everywhere.

The teams were divided into two groups, A and B. In Group A England and New Zealand got through to the semi-final, and in Group B West Indies and Australia. But West Indies only just beat Pakistan in the closest match of the competition, winning by one wicket off the fourth ball of the last over. But they had a surprisingly easy victory over Australia by seven wickets thanks largely to a sensational innings of 78 by Kallicharran who scored 35 off his last ten balls from Lillee.

In the semi-finals, England, top of Group A, played Australia, the second team of Group B. On a green pitch England were put into bat and found the fast left-arm deliveries of Gary Gilmour unplayable. With a devastating late inswinger he took 6 for 14 and England could only make 93 off 36.2 overs. But Australia found the conditions just as difficult and lost six wickets with Gary Gilmour top scorer with 28 not out before they won by four wickets.

In the other semi-final West Indies beat New Zealand

easily by five wickets which meant they would meet
Australia in the final at Lords. And what a match it proved
to be, watched by twenty-six thousand with the gates closed.
It continued uninterrupted except for the intervals from 11
am to 8.43 pm. This made it probably the longest-ever day in
cricket of this class. The famous Gillette semi-final between
Lancashire and Gloucestershire at Old Trafford in 1971
started at the same time and didn't finish until 8.50 pm. But
this included an hour's delay because of rain at lunchtime.
But luckily the Prudential final was on 21 June – the longest
day in the year – so the light held and Prince Philip presented the Prudential Cup to the worthy winners – West
Indies. Thanks almost entirely to a superb innings of 102 by
their captain Clive Lloyd they made 291 for 8 off their 60
overs. In reply Australia were 274 all out off 58.4 overs, but
when all seemed inevitably lost nearly brought off a dramatic victory thanks to a last-wicket stand of 41 between that
dynamic speed duo Lillee and Thomson. It really was a
wonderful match and set the seal on the competition, which
was such a success that there was universal clamour for a
repeat as soon as possible. It also gave me an opportunity
for a nickname which I could not resist. Eighteen-year-old
Javed Miandad just had to become Javed Mumandi.

After the severe drubbing which England had received
during the winter in Australia, not even their most optimistic
supporter could have expected them to win the four-match
Test series against Australia, which had been laid on at short
notice to fill the gap after the Prudential Cup was over. In
fact Australia only won 1–0, and their victory in the First
Test at Edgbaston was largely due to Mike Denness' decision to put them into bat when he won the toss. Poor Mike!
He had seemed to have salvaged some of his reputation as a
captain and player after England's Test victories at Melbourne and Auckland, to which he contributed scores of 188
and 181. But the morning of 10 July at Edgbaston was dull
and grey, and Mike after consultation with his team took a
gamble and lost. It is now known that it *was* a team decision
though of course the responsibility was Mike's. But Snow
and Arnold especially fancied their chances against the
Australian batsmen, expecting that the damp heavy

atmosphere would give them movement in the air and off the pitch. At the same time the most cynical of the pundits thought that the decision might have been slightly influenced by the wish to avoid meeting Lillee, Walker and Thomson in conditions which should favour the bowlers at least before lunch.

As it turned out, the England bowlers got no movement off the pitch nor in the air, though at one time Australia, at 186 for 5, were struggling a bit. But thanks to some solid and consistent batting (Marsh's 61 was top score) they reached 359. Not a winning score and one which Denness might well have settled for at the start of the match. But the gods don't like captains who put the other side in. As soon as Edrich and Amiss opened for England so did the heavens for Australia, and a terrific thunderstorm flooded the ground. Edrich (34) was top scorer, the next highest being Knott with 14 and England were all out for 101, Lillee and Walker getting unpleasant lift and movement out of the damp pitch. England following on 258 runs behind were 93 for 5 at the close on Saturday night. After further thunderstorms on Monday they were all out 173 – beaten by an innings and 85 runs with a day and a half to spare. Mike Denness of course became the scapegoat and the media brayed for his blood. In fact by the Friday evening he had already told the selectors that he was ready to stand down in view of what had happened.

Naturally the statisticians had a field day. At least so far as England is concerned W. G. Grace seems to have been right, when he once said, 'After winning the toss, by all means think about putting the other side in. Then think again and invariably decide to bat.' Including Edgbaston, England captains have put Australia in to bat on eleven occasions, and have only won once – in Melbourne under J. W. H. T. Douglas in 1912. They have lost eight times, the three which perhaps most of us remember being Len Hutton at Brisbane in 1954, Peter May at Adelaide in 1959 and Tony Greig in the Centenary Test at Melbourne in 1977.

Australia's captains have done a little better after putting England into bat on twelve occasions. They have won three and lost five. If you were to ask Richie Benaud today, I'm pretty certain he would give you much the same advice as W.G. But he himself did in fact win two out of these three victories, both at Melbourne – against England in 1959, and West Indies in 1961, the other being by Monty Noble at Lord's in 1909. But I am equally sure that Richie would say that, knowing the conditions and the fine bowlers he had to take advantage of them, his two decisions were NOT gambles.

But to go back to the Edgbaston disaster. It is unfair to put the entire blame for England's defeat on Mike Denness' decision. First of all Lillee and Walker with seven wickets apiece, and Thomson with five, all bowled well except for some waywardness by Thomson in the first innings. They took full advantage of the conditions and were backed by superbly aggressive fielding. It was also obvious that some of our batsmen were still shell-shocked from the battering they had received in Australia. For instance, poor Dennis Amiss, whose last three Test scores against Australia had been 0, 0, 0, made 4 and 5, also suffered a sickening blow on the left elbow.

The other disappointment was a 'pair' for the twenty-one-year-old Essex batsman Graham Gooch, playing in his first Test. Only the week before at Lord's he had made a fine attacking 75 against the Australians. But this time he received an unplayable ball in the first innings, pitching on a good length middle and off and leaving him late off the pitch. He snicked it to Marsh and brought forth the inevitable cliché from all of us in the commentary box that a less gifted batsman would not have been good enough to touch it. Cliché maybe, but true for all that.

But whatever the excuses or reasons, no one could deny that England had got off to a disastrous start and that changes including the captaincy had to be made. So for the Second Test at Lord's Tony Greig was appointed captain, and the selectors decided to try batsmen known to be good against fast bowling – somewhat obvious perhaps! Anyhow in place of Denness and Fletcher, Barry Wood and David Steele were brought in, plus allrounder Bob Woolmer in place of Chris Old. Wood is a small gutsy player at his best against speed, and the surprise selection Steele, a front-foot player with great powers of determination and concentration. But more of him when we get to Lord's.

Before ·leaving Edgbaston I must relate an amusing experience we had in the commentary box there. During one of the breaks in play due to the thunderstorms, we were having one of our usual discussions in the box rather than return to the studio for music. It was a hot sultry afternoon and for some reason we were discussing how cricket seemed to run in families. I suggested that this was often due to an enthusiastic mum who was prepared to play cricket in the garden with her sons. I quoted Penny Cowdrey, whose three boys are all following in Colin's footsteps. I said that only the week before she had taken five wickets against the Junior Boys XI of her youngest son Graham's preparatory school at Broadstairs. I then added mischievously: 'Yes, they tell me that on that day her swingers were practically unplayable.'

As I had suspected, this remark started everyone in the box giggling. Under some difficulties we continued the discussion and mentioned Vic Richardson's daughter who for years bowled for her three sons Ian, Greg and Trevor Chappell. Don Mosey said Trevor was having a wonderful season in the Lancashire League and that people were saying he would eventually be better than either Ian or Greg. I added that he had already played for South Australia but that I thought he had lost his place in their side last season. 'Anyway,' I went on with confidence, knowing that Alan Mac-Gilvray was at the back of the box, 'we've got just the chap to confirm this. Alan . . .'

I turned round and saw that Alan was fast asleep, chin resting deep on his chest, with a slight whistling sound coming down his nose. This set us all off laughing again, but to cover up and save Alan any embarrassment I managed to blurt out: 'I'm sorry, I'm afraid Alan must have left the box.' With that Alan woke up with a snort and a start and said: 'What's going on? What do you want to know?' But by then we were helpless with laughter and couldn't tell him. All the listeners could hear was a gentle hissing and sobbing as we tried to stem our laughter. Nobody spoke for at least ten seconds, and that is a long time on the air. Don Mosey, who is the worst giggler of the lot, managed to make a bolt for the door, and collapsed outside, leaving me to hold the fort.

When I was able to talk I came clean with the listeners and admitted that Alan had indeed been caught napping! This so far as I am concerned has been the only occasion in thirty years of broadcasting when I have seen a box of commentators silenced by their laughter. The only other similar occasion – which I have described before – was when I was doing a radio broadcast at Hove on a match between Sussex and Hampshire. Henry Horton was playing for Hampshire and he had this funny sort of stance at the wicket with his bottom stuck out. I thought I ought to explain this to the listeners so said: 'Horton has a funny sort of stance,' and then *meant* to say – 'it looks as if he's sitting on a shooting stick.' BUT I got it the wrong way round! Then although I myself managed to keep going, for the first and only time I saw a scorer – Michael Fordham – having to leave the box because he was so hysterical with laughter.

To get back to the Second Test at Lord's, Tony Greig personally got off to a great start in his new role as England's captain. After four wickets had fallen to Lillee for only 49 runs, he made an aggressive 96. His first partner in this rescue act was the newcomer David Steele. With his grey hair and steel spectacles he was a most unlikely figure to bat No. 3 for England, and to have to face the speed and fire of Lillee and Thomson. But in addition to his normal forward defensive stroke, he attacked anything short with superb hooks and cuts. He made a fine 50 before being bowled by Thomson, and the crowd rose to him. They had taken him to their heart and in this one short innings he suddenly became a national hero – the plain Mr Everybody who dared to stand up to Lillee. People felt they could identify themselves with him, since in his appearance he was more like someone you'd expect to see in a solicitor's office than a Test cricketer.

More support came from Alan Knott with a typical 69 and England made 315. Snow then bowled beautifully and Australia were all out for 268. In the second innings Edrich and Wood put on 111 for the first wicket – a rare luxury for England – Edrich finished with 175 – the second highest innings against Australia at Lord's. England batted with far more assurance and confidence and Greig was able to declare at 436 for 7 setting Australia 484 to win. All except poor Dennis Amiss (10) made useful scores and Steele once again played bravely and sensibly for 45. In the end Australia by dogged batting reached 329 for 3, but it was an honorable draw, and a match which Greig could look back on with great personal satisfaction. It was not just his own scores of 96 and 41 but his flamboyant captaincy seemed to give new spirit to the England team.

This, alas, was to be the end of the road – temporarily only as it turned out – for Amiss. He obviously needed a rest from the battering of Lillee and Thomson who always seemed to keep something especially nasty up their sleeves for him. Equally sad was that Graham Gooch in spite of 31 in the second innings was dropped by the selectors for the Third Test – yet another case of a young attacking batsman being shed after far too short a trial in Test cricket. Shades of Colin Milburn!

It had been mighty hot at Lord's with the temperature in the nineties. In the Long Room of the Pavilion even the most traditional members removed their jackets and ties, much to the 'distress' of the Secretariat. But they did not go quite as far as a gentleman in front of the Tavern. For a bet he removed all but his plimsolls and socks and 'streaked' on to the field during a break in play. He ran across towards the grandstand, and then turned right-handed and ran down the length of the pitch towards the Nursery End, doing the splits over both sets of stumps. It was of course a 'first' at Lord's which was the last place one would have expected it to happen. I suppose I should have disapproved but I must admit I thought it gloriously funny and that it fitted into the gala atmosphere of the packed, sun-drenched Lord's. The streaker did it very delicately and no play was interfered with. The police led him gently away to loud applause and much laughter from the huge crowd.

The next day, the magistrate fined him the amount of his bet which left him with a small profit from what he got out of interviews with the Press. They splashed his photograph

across their front pages, showing his backside as he cleared
the stumps. In private I was shown the full frontal photograph which the Press did NOT publish! Alan Knott was
batting at the time and standing down by the stumps at the
Nursery End. He told me later that as the streaker ran
towards him it was the first time he had ever seen *two* balls
coming down the pitch at him! Needless to say my poet
friend Les Bailey of Wombwell turned up trumps and sent
me this poem:

> *He ran on in his birthday attire*
> *Setting the ladies aflame with desire.*
> *But when he came to the stumps*
> *He misjudged his jumps —*
> *Now he sings in the Luton Girl's Choir!*

In between the Tests I took part in two unusual events. First
of all Guinness sponsored a competition for throwing the
cricket ball, which was televised by London Weekend. It
took place after a day's racing in front of the grandstand at
Sandown Park. A number of first-class cricketers and club
cricketers took part, and the object was to see if anyone could
beat the ninety-one-year-old record made by Richard Percival in 1884. He threw a ball 140 yards 2 feet – an incredible
distance, and funnily enough he also did it on a racecourse at
Durham.

Everyone had three throws but no one got anywhere near the
record. The winner was John Lever of Essex with 107 yards 8
inches, second was Majid Khan 106 yards 1 foot 3 inches and
third Keith Boyce 106 yards 1 foot 1 inch. Boyce in one of the
practice throws the competitors were allowed before racing
began actually threw 120 yards but possibly the long wait
affected him and the others. But whatever the reason I was
surprised that no one could get nearer than 34 yards to the
old record. In almost all other athletic sports such as running, jumping, swimming and so on there has been regular
improvement in performances, with records being smashed
year after year. Perhaps – dare I say it – Mr Percival's
record was not made under such close and careful scrutiny as
we had at Sandown Park.

There is one other possible explanation. Our short boundaries of about 75 yards mean that our cricketers are not required to throw long distances. One day cricket has improved the speed and accuracy of throwing beyond belief but not the distance. Unfortunately no member of the Australian touring team was allowed to compete for fear of injury to their shoulders. Otherwise someone like Doug Walters or Jeff Thomson would almost certainly have won, because with boundaries of 100 yards or more on Australian grounds they have the need to throw further, and get the necessary practice.

The other event was a nostalgic one for me and I hope for quite a few listeners too. Aeolian Hall in Bond Street, which had been the home of BBC Radio Light Entertainment for many years, was being closed down. To mark the occasion Radio 2 decided to mount a special edition of the old *In Town Tonight* programme. It was broadcast 'live' in the actual studio from which *In Town Tonight* used originally to come, and in addition there were three or four points outside in various parts of London. John Ellison – the old presenter of *In Town Tonight* – was in Piccadilly Circus doing interviews with passers-by, Pete Murray was up in Big Ben and I was in a sauna bath in Kensington. It was quite like the old days of *Let's Go Somewhere*, the spot I used to do in the programme from 1948–52. Radio 2 paid three visits to me – in the hot room, under the cold shower, and being 'slapped' on the massage table – all of them naturally accompanied by my usual giggles and shouts. It was twenty-three years since I had done a similar programme, and I must admit at least *I* enjoyed it.

At the time too it was a happy occasion for my old friend John Ellison. He had been seriously ill for the past year or two and came back especially to do this broadcast, in the programme which he had introduced for so many years. But sadly it was his last broadcast as he died a short time later. Besides being a great friend of mine, John had taken me under his wing when I first joined the BBC in 1946, and I learnt much of what I know today about radio from him, especially in the art of interviewing. He was a really professional radio performer with great charm and an ability to get on with people. Someone once described him as the commentator with the smile in his voice – a well-deserved epitaph.

The Third Test at Headingley in August made cricket history. It was the first Test ever to be abandoned because of vandals as opposed to rioters or bottle throwers. England went into the match greatly heartened by their performance at Lord's which had given their morale a much-needed fillip. The selectors made four changes, poor Amiss being spared another confrontation with Lillee and Thomson. He was replaced by John Hampshire on his home ground. He was currently in good form and always at his best against fast bowling, but lacked consistency. Even so he had been rather unfairly ignored by the selectors since making 107 against West Indies at Lord's on his debut in 1969 – since then he had only played in seven Tests.

The other batsman to be dropped was Graham Gooch, which to many seemed a cowardly and retrograde step. If he had been good enough to be chosen for the First Test it was surely much too early to discard him after only four innings. Three were admittedly failures, though his first 0 at Edgbaston was the result of an unplayable ball. But his 31 at Lord's was sound enough even if lacking his usual aggression. To replace him the selectors made the astonishing choice of Keith Fletcher – if you believe in the concept of horses for courses. Headingley had been his unlucky ground ever since he had been picked instead of Phil Sharpe in 1968 against the Australians and then promptly dropped three catches at slip, which the Yorkshire crowd thought that Sharpe would have gobbled up. As poor Fletcher followed these misses with a 0 he has not been given much of a reception at Headingley ever since!

Edmonds and Old came in for Woolmer and Lever, so unusually England went into a Test with two front-line left-arm bowlers. This time the selectors were proved right as the pitch was slow and easy paced and took a certain amount of spin almost from the start. Greig won the toss and England struggled to 288 thanks to the doggedness of Edrich (62) and that man Steele again (73). The only bright batting came from Greig with an aggressive 51. Australia could only make 135 in reply thanks to a sensational Test debut by Phil Edmonds, who in his first twelve overs in Test cricket took 5 for 17 – he finished with 20–7–28–5 compared with Underwood's 19–12–22–1.

In their second innings England managed to muster 291, thanks inevitably to Steele (92) who once again combined grim forward defence with the occasional four off the shorter balls, and once actually straight drove Mallett for 6 which shook everyone. Incidentally, his runs for England earned him a lifetime's supply of lamb chops and steaks from a local butcher who sponsored Steele with a chop for every run up to fifty, and a steak for each run after that. The failures of Hampshire (14 and 0) and Fletcher (8 and 14) confirmed that the selectors' policy of chop and change in order to follow the men in form seldom pays off. At least they could not have done *much* worse by leaving Woolmer and Gooch in the side and by so doing have given some encouragement to youth.

Australia were set the 'impossible' task of scoring 445 to win. At that time only Australia with 404 in the Headingley Test of 1948 had made more than 400 to win in the fourth innings of a Test. But thanks to McCosker (95 not out) and Ian Chappell (62) by close of play Australia were 220 for 3, and so only needed 225 with seven wickets in hand to win. One of the reasons for their success was the change in the bowling of Edmonds. His nagging accuracy of the first innings deserted him and he bowled far too many balls outside the leg-stump. At any rate the game was beautifully poised, with both sides having good reason to think that they could win.

This made the abandonment of play on the last day all the sadder at the time, though as it turned out heavy drizzle from mid-morning onwards would have prevented play anyway. The first I heard of the vandalism was when I was woken up at my hotel by a telephone call from the *Today* programme. They told me what had happened and asked me to comment. Naturally I was disgusted and angry that cricket had once again been made the scapegoat of politics. I recalled some of the other Tests in which pitches had been interfered with. There was Lord's in 1926 when a hosepipe had flooded the pitch but no one ever discovered who had turned it on or left it on. On Len Hutton's tour of Australia the Melbourne pitch was found to have been mysteriously watered when play was resumed after the weekend. I had of course also been present when play was interrupted by bottle-throwers at Sabina Park during Cowdrey's tour and for the famous Illingworth walk-off at Sydney. There were also other bottle-throwing incidents which interrupted play in the West Indies on both Hutton's and May's tours. But the only other complete abandonment of a match due to anything other than weather was the Karachi Test in 1969. Here the crowd invaded the pitch and set fire to the stands with Alan Knott 96 not out on the way to his first Test hundred. On this occasion players, Press and broadcasters had to take refuge in the pavilion, before being smuggled out of the ground – twelve to a car! We all packed our bags and flew back to England that same night.

The damage to the Headingley pitch was not severe. There was some crude oil on a good length and some holes dug with a knife near the batting crease. But it was sufficient to make play out of the question, as it would have been grossly unfair to restart the match on a newly cut pitch, unaffected by the wear and tear of four days' cricket. The culprits were caught and one of them served a thirteen-month prison sentence. Ironically, as I've said, because of rain their action had no affect on the result of the match but it did give them the publicity they wanted for their cause – the release of a colleague from prison. Unfortunately, it cost cricket at least five thousand pounds and could have ruined what was certain to be a really exciting Test.

The Fourth and final Test at the Oval also earned its place in cricket history. It was the longest game of cricket ever played in England, lasting the full six days and ending as late as 3 September – the only time I can remember a Test Match in September. Our selectors admitted their mistake at Headingley and dropped Fletcher and Hampshire, bringing back Woolmer and re-introducing Roope to Test cricket after an absence of two years. Ian Chappell won the toss for the first time in the series on what was to be a slow pitch throughout. After being robbed of his hundred by the vandals at Headingley when he was 95 not out, McCosker made his maiden Test century and Ian Chappell, in his last Test as Australian captain, made a typically aggressive 192 and was able to declare at 532 for 9. For some reason which I have never discovered he treated the packed Oval crowd with contempt and discourtesy, failing to acknowledge in any way the generous applause for his hundred or the acclamation he received on returning to the pavilion. An unnecessary display of bad manners which would, I know, have greatly shocked his grandfather, that great sportsman Vic Richardson.

England as at Edgbaston got the worst of the weather, and during their first innings of 191 had to struggle against drizzle, interruptions, heavy cloud and bad light. Lillee (2), Thomson (4) and Walker (4) took full advantage of the conditions, and the inevitable Steele was top scorer with 39. Following on 341 runs behind there was only one thing for England to do – to get their heads down and fight for a draw. And this, with grim determination and plenty of guts, they proceeded to do. The newcomer Roope (77) and Woolmer (149) justified the selectors' choice, and need I say it Steele (66) again 'came good' and brought his final figures in his first ever Test series to:

Inns	N.O.	Runs	Top Score	Average
6	0	365	92	60.83

Remarkable. Those two great England stalwarts Edrich (96) and Knott (64) were other big contributors to England's second innings' score of 538.

There were only eighty-five minutes left for Australia to try to make 198 to win, and they made 40 for 2 before stumps were pulled up half an hour early. The real winner of the game was Harry Brind's pitch in his first Test as groundsman at The Oval. It was far too slow, but remained true and showed no sign of breaking up. The short series of four Tests had been a great success, the cricket, the crowds and the weather all helping to make the 1975 cricket season one to remember. Australia deserved to win the series because they took their chance when it was offered them at Edgbaston.

England could console themselves that thanks largely to the lack of pace and bounce in our pitches they had wiped the slate clean after their annihilation in Australia, and but for the weather might have squared the series.

Just three last memories of the Oval Test. Bob Woolmer's hundred was the slowest ever by an England batsman against Australia. It took him 6 hours 34 minutes against the previous slowest 6 hours 2 minutes by Colin Cowdrey at Sydney in 1959. Secondly, on the Saturday when the light was at its worst we were all surprised that the umpires Dicky Bird and Tom Spencer did not stop play for bad light. So evidently was John Snow, who kept casting long glances at the dark clouds and making it quite obvious that he found it difficult to see out in the middle. When he realised his hints were being ignored he decided on more drastic tactics. He hit Walker over mid-off for 4, and then gave him 'the charge' and lofted him over long on for another 4. This was followed by a cross-batted stroke for 2 to mid wicket – 10 runs off the over, the most expensive of the day. Then surprise surprise, immediately it was over the umpires conferred and declared that the light was unfit! We couldn't help wondering how many runs Snow might have made had the light been good!

Finally I was given an opportunity for one of my more preposterous puns. Trevor Bailey was discussing whether England should have taken more risks in their second innings in order to score more quickly. If they did, of course, there was the danger of their losing wickets. 'It's very difficult to strike a happy medium', he said. 'You *could* go to a séance,' I butted in, ducking the sweets and bits of paper flung at me by my long-suffering colleagues.

I know that I am biased but I have always found that cricketers in general are very nice people. There's something about the game perhaps which helps to build character, tolerance and humour. The modern first-class cricketer is no exception and I am extremely grateful to them all for the way they have always given me – and continue to give – their friendship.

I have only one complaint against them. I wish they could look as if they were enjoying themselves more. How seldom do you see them smiling or laughing *on* the field. Yet I know that almost all of them love cricket and are sacrificing quite a lot of money to play it. But I fear the pressure and the pace of the present crowded season has made their cricket too much like a job of work. For them it's like going to the office or factory every morning. It's not that they really *play* too much cricket. But the constant dashing from place to place up the motorways is an exhausting business. They have to do it to fit in all the different types of competitions.

It is possible for someone to finish a three-day County Championship match on a Friday, travel somewhere to play a one-day Benson and Hedges on the Saturday and be off again somewhere else on the Sunday for a one-day John Player match.

Sometimes, if there has been rain on the Saturday, a cricketer will have to go back to finish the Benson and Hedges on the Monday or Tuesday. It could even happen that he then has to report for a five-day Test Match on the Wednesday. Four different types of cricket in one week, with of course the Gillette Cup to come later in the season. It's a wonder they know which game they are playing with all the different rules and regulations.

And of course it sometimes happens that a batsman is not out in a county match on the Saturday evening, has to play a new innings in the John Player on Sunday and then go back to continue the not out innings on Monday. However much anyone loves cricket it is not surprising that it sometimes seems too much of a good thing to the county cricketers. But of course this applies to almost everything in life. The less you have the more you appreciate it when you do have it, as this following story illustrates:

There was a professor lecturing to a group of men on the subject of sex, and he asked his audience if they would help him. Would those who made love to their wives *every* night please hold up their hands? Then those who made it every other night, twice a week, once a week, once a month and so on. Each time the men rather sheepishly held up their hands at the number which concerned them. Finally, after he had counted each category, the professor said: 'Thank you for your help. That's all.' But a small man right at the back of the hall held up his hand and with a cheerful smile said: 'Excuse me, sir, you haven't asked me yet.' 'All right,' said the professor impatiently, 'how often do *you* do it?' 'Once a year,' replied the small man still smiling. 'Well, what are you looking so pleased about?' asked the professor. 'It's tonight,' replied the small man. See what I mean?

Sixth Over Alarums and excursions

In September 1975 Pauline and I went to Corfu for a fortnight's holiday and were lucky enough to enjoy cloudless blue skies and hot sunshine throughout our stay. We went with a party organised by *Cricketer* magazine and stayed in the Cricketer Taverna situated among the olive groves and cypress trees on the west side of Corfu. It is a beautiful island, far lusher and greener than we had expected with majestic mountains and quiet secluded beaches and coves. We visited these in a caique belonging to Ben and Belinda Brocklehurst – the *Cricketer* hosts. We used to chug our way along the deserted west coast until we found a peaceful spot with not a living soul in sight.

When we were not swimming or sunbathing we went to the picturesque cricket ground right in the centre of Corfu Town. Cricket has been played in Corfu for over 160 years and was first introduced there by the Royal Navy. The ground has been greatly improved in recent years and the outfield is now of coarse grass with a matting pitch. The Greeks are up to good club standard in bowling and fielding but their batting would be no good on an English grass pitch. But out there on the matting with its bounce they get away with some crude cross-batted strokes. What they lack in skill they make up for in enthusiasm and courage, cheered on by the shouts and applause of the large crowds which sit under the trees around the ground, sipping cool drinks brought by waiters from the nearby cafés.

There are usually matches every Wednesday, Saturday and Sunday, and at the weekend there are often three to four thousand people watching. There were two local Greek teams when we were there, now there are three. Our two were Gymnasticos and Byron, who play each other and visiting teams from England and Holland, who usually spend a fortnight on the island. There are also occasional matches against BEA and the Royal Navy. Somehow there always seemed to be exciting finishes with the excitement and uproar worthy of a Wembley Cup Final. I was persuaded to play in one match for the *Cricketer* against Gymnasticos and going in No. 11 made a stylish single down to third man before being caught in the gully. But at least I can say I have played in Corfu.

Although extremely brave when batting – often without gloves – and in attempting impossible stops or catches, the Greeks tend to kick up a tremendous fuss when they *are* hurt. A batsman hit almost anywhere will lie down moaning and drumming his legs on the ground. One of their batsmen was hit in a match against the Old Wellingtonians who, with a team made up from the *Cricketer* readers, were staying at our Taverna. The bowler was their volatile captain – Christopher Brown, son of Freddie Brown and a fast and highly dangerous bowler on the matting. As usual the batsman collapsed groaning on the ground, and various spectators rushed out to attend to him. But he lay there writhing in apparent agony, so a call was made for any doctor in the crowd.

In the Old Wellingtonian party was a young medical student in his first year at a teaching hospital. He wasn't selected for this match, so got up from his deckchair in the shade and went out to try and help. He approached the injured man, knelt down and asked him where he was hurt. Between his groans the man muttered something in Greek and pointed to his left ankle, which when the sock was rolled down, was sure enough badly bruised and looking a nasty mess. But the young Wellingtonian rose to his feet without doing anything. 'I am sorry,' he said, 'I haven't got down that far yet in my studies,' and walked back to his seat.

One day, when watching, I was looking through an old scorebook on the scorers' table. You won't believe this, but I do assure you the Greeks have some rather unusual names. I found that in one match a batsman from a visiting English team was out: stumped Penis Bowled Crabsarse!

Back from our holiday in Corfu, I had a very busy autumn. There was the new way of recording *Down Your Way*, doing two in the first week of the month, two in the second week, leaving the last half of the month free. There were the usual number of talks, lectures and dinners and commentary on the Lord Mayor's Show for television. There was also a very special occasion for me when the Sheffield Cricket Lovers' Soceity gave a dinner in my honour. My old friend Don Mosey proposed my health and I still blush at the kind tribute on the front of the menu.

> *To Brian*
> *As a token of our appreciation*
> *for the pleasure you have given*
> *cricket lovers the world over.*

Could anything be nicer than that? It did much to allay the guilty feeling I often have that a large slice of my life has been taken up with describing a piece of leather being hit by a piece of wood. It also made me – a southerner – feel very humble and grateful to my wife's home county, Yorkshire. To date I have had two dinners given in my honour and both have been in Yorkshire – at Wombwell and Sheffield. And, you know, it's always rightly said that Yorkshiremen know their cricket!

As Christmas approached we had one of those domestic crises which crop up in every family. For about six years Pauline had had a dodgy back and had undergone treatment on it from time to time. At the end of November it suddenly 'went', and her specialist decided that complete rest might stave off an operation. So for eight weeks she was on her back in bed which, with me away so often, brought quite a few complications in our life. But everyone rallied round and the Red Cross did a marvellous job in helping to ferry our youngest daughter Joanna to and from her school bus in Islington. They were all volunteers who gave up their spare time to help and only charged the bare minimum to pay for their petrol.

We had also sent out invitations to a Meet the Neighbours Party. After nearly thirty years in St John's Wood we felt we knew many of our neighbours – some intimately, some on a nodding acquaintance. But we wondered how many of them knew one another so we sent out fifty invitations and only had one refusal! I naturally wanted to cancel the whole thing, but Pauline pleaded for it to go ahead. So go ahead it did with Pauline holding court in our bedroom. It was voted a great success and as a result we hope that quite a few neighbours know each other better.

With three of the family – Clare, Andrew and Ian – all in Sydney, Barry, Joanna, Pauline and I – plus of course Cally and Mini – had our turkey and plum pudding round the bedside from where we telephoned the others in Australia, which cost a little matter of twenty-one pounds by the time everyone had had their say! An unusual, rather expensive but happy Christmas.

But back to backs! It's amazing how many people in all walks of life do suffer from a bad back and it is a great temptation to take their advice. They all seem to have a miracle man round the corner who has cured them by some magic manipulation. Unfortunately most people add: 'You simply *must* go to him. He's wonderful. I've been to him for years.' Not much of an advertisement for his healing powers if it means constant attendance!

But rest worked wonders with Pauline and by January she was up and about and gradually returned to normal – until that fateful Easter Saturday. It was one of those days. On the Good Friday Pauline had swung a gentle golf club and suffered no pain nor seemingly any after-effects. My son Barry was busy arranging a party for his birthday the next day. On the Saturday we were all going to the local point to point and the stew – our staple diet on these occasions – had been cooked in readiness. I woke to hear a whisper from Pauline saying that her back had gone again, and that she was in great pain and could not move. She had those old shooting pains up the left thigh and leg. I rushed out to the doctor's to get some pain-killing pills and returned to find that four out of Barry's six guests had rung to say they could not come to his party. Pauline insisted that we all went to the point to point, leaving her behind with rations for the day by her bed, though she could just stagger on all fours to the bathroom. Looking back it all looks rather heartless but it was a gorgeous spring day and all she wanted was to be left in peace to lie quietly on her back.

Anyway, we packed up the boot of my car with the stews, bottles, picnic basket, binoculars, rugs, etc, and as it was such a nice day I took off my coat and flung it into the boot which I then closed. We all got into the car, and prepared to move off. Everyone was laughing and joking but suddenly I froze in my seat and sat motionless. I suddenly realised that my ignition key was in the ticket pocket of my coat which was now inside the boot, which was self-locking. I wouldn't say that I remained calm – in fact I ran through the first few chapters of my book of expletives. But I then remembered how friendly were the Swanage police, so rang them for help. Sure enough within minutes a little white panda car came tearing up the road and a PC got out dangling an enormous bunch of car keys! Relief! Surely there must be one similar to mine among them. But try as we could, we were unable to find one to fit. We tried some of them twice but after twenty minutes or so we gave up. Then we had our first bit of luck. A friend from across the way came over and said he knew a chap in the nearby hotel who was a Ford dealer. So we went to find him and though he hadn't got any keys he told us that if you remove the back seat of a Ford it is just possible to put an arm through a narrow gap into the boot. So Barry did this and after much grunting and groaning managed to retrieve my coat. We were saved, but our troubles were not over yet. Just as we were finally about to set off the telephone rang and it was the remaining two of Barry's guests saying they couldn't come to his party. So that was off, we were leaving Pauline in pain upstairs, we were going to miss the first race and when we got there we failed to back a single winner. As I said, it was one of those days!

The next week was taken up with trying to save Pauline's back. The local GP recommended gentle physiotherapy, and before contacting her own specialist in London we decided to try one final 'miracle' man in Bournemouth, who had been recommended by friends. 'One finger on the spot and hey presto – the disc will slip back into place.' After examining Pauline he said: 'Twenty years ago I would have put you straight on the table and manipulated you. Almost certainly

I would have cured you – at least temporarily. But now I am not so impetuous. I know the risk of failure, even though it is ever so slight. So I fear that there is nothing that I can do for you.'

So off we went to London and after another examination our London back specialist said there was nothing for it but to operate, which he duly did and removed *two* discs. There followed three months or so of painful convalescence, including a stay at the delightful Osborne House in the Isle of Wight. The back seemed all right but there were still the shooting pains down the side of the leg. But the specialist was calmly confident that all would be well in the end. And touch wood, after three months of gentle exercises the pain gradually disappeared, and Pauline's back was cured. I have gone into all this with some detail to show that there is some hope for back sufferers, even if it does mean an operation in the end. But don't expect an immediate cure and try to resist the advice of well-meaning friends whose little man round the corner will cure you at a touch. I know such people exist but there *is* a risk attached to it and you could be the one for whom the magic touch does harm.

In January 1976 we had a heartening occasion involving the Metropolitan Police. At the time there were quite a few advertisements on TV encouraging children in trouble at home to dial the police on 999. One Sunday after lunch Pauline and I were drinking our coffee in the sitting-room when Cally came in and said there were two policemen walking *down* the stairs from the floor above where we and Joanna have our bedrooms.

Somewhat surprised, I went out and saw the two soft-capped policemen coming down. I asked them what they were doing and what they wanted. They were very nice and explained that they had come in answer to a 999 call from a Joanna Johnston of 98 Hamilton Terrace. They received the call when shadowing a procession which was making its way slowly down Oxford Street. So, much relieved at getting some real action, they pulled out all the stops and raced up to St John's Wood in about two minutes flat with blue light flashing and siren wailing. Before they could even ring our bell, they were admitted by our Entry-com which operates from the second and third floors.

Joanna, who had obviously been on the lookout for them, invited them in, and when they reached her floor, burst into tears. So they were coming down to find someone who could explain what was going on. We all rushed upstairs to find poor Joanna sobbing her heart out on our bed obviously overcome with what she had done. The police were wonderful. They talked quietly to her, gave her their Christian names and told her all about their car which they said was the fastest in the fleet. They went on to say that whenever she *was* in trouble it was quite right to dial 999 but if Joanna just wanted to talk to a policeman she could ring 935 1113 which was Marylebone Lane Police Station, and they would be very happy to speak to her.

Under this sympathetic approach Joanna soon perked up and explained that she had seen the TV advertisement, and wanted to see what happened. She promised not to do it again and, here comes the best part, the policemen took her down, put her in the back of their car and drove her up Hamilton Terrace and back at great speed, with siren wailing, and lights flashing. It was certainly a day which she will never forget and I wrote a letter to the Chief Superintendent at Marylebone Lane. I apologised for the trouble caused and praised the behaviour and understanding of the two officers. I added that it was so nice to be able to bowl a gentle half-volley at the police, instead of the usual bumper which they normally received from the public. He replied that he had shown my letter to the two officers and that they appreciated 'the friendly ball instead of the usual body-line, and are encouraged to return to the crease on another occasion'. Who says our policemen are *not* wonderful?

Ever since Pauline and I were married way back in 1948 we have always had a dog. We started with my favourite breed – a Sealyham with a black eye called Smokey. The last dog I had had before the war was also a Sealyham called Blob who adored cricket and used to sit on the boundary quite happily with ears pricked watching us play. Smokey was a lady and wasn't so keen. But she was a great character though not too intelligent. But she was clever enough to produce five super puppies and made a perfect mother. She had a loathing for cats. This was a pity as she was perfectly trained and would sit immediately on command except when she spotted a cat. She would then give instant chase regardless of traffic. So this unfortunately meant that she always had to be on a lead when going for a walk.

Smokey lived to the ripe old age of thirteen and we then had Bonny, a King Charles Spaniel, very highly strung and far too friendly with everyone. We sold him after a few months and he was replaced by Mini – a miniature Yorkshire terrier. Pauline saw her looking miserable in a pet shop window and took pity on her and bought her on the spot. Thank goodness Pauline did. Mini is the sweetest character, supersensitive to a change of voice and very obedient. Yorkies are very tough, will walk for miles and make wonderful companions. She delights in chasing cats and squirrels who invade the garden but never does so away from her own territory. Because she is so obedient she never needs a lead, not even in busy streets. She stays close to heel and at the word 'stay' stands rigidly still So at a crossing she stands waiting for the word 'over' but if by chance a motorist turns across the lights another 'stay' will act on Mini like high powered brakes and she comes to a dead stop.

We haven't been so lucky with our other pets. We had hamsters who regularly used to lie down and die at the exact end of their two-year life cycle. Then there was poor old Fred the tortoise. One year as usual in late October he dug himself down in one of our flower beds to hibernate. Unfortunately January that year was freakishly hot and to our amazement one day we saw a very dishevelled and dirty Fred moving slowly across the lawn. He had mistakenly thought that spring had come. We rang a local pet shop to ask what we ought to do as we feared frost and snow would soon return and he would die of cold. The man suggested putting Fred into the fridge for a short time to make him think it really was winter and time to re-hibernate. We thought this sounded too drastic so asked the Zoo's advice. They weren't very hopeful. They recommended putting him in a basket full of straw with some food and water and trust that he would go off to sleep again. We did this, but the Zoo were right. It didn't succeed and poor Fred never went off to sleep again and died presumably of cold.

We had no better luck with two budgies who caught a chill and died, so it's just as well we were not professional zoo keepers. At a dinner I once heard a Welsh clergyman tell an unlikely story about budgies. A man had bought two from a pet shop but was annoyed that he couldn't tell which was the male or the female. So he went back to the shop and asked how he could find out.

'Oh, it's quite easy,' said the owner of the pet shop. 'Creep quietly downstairs in the middle of the night and see if you can catch them making love. When they do, seize the one on top and tie a piece of cotton round its neck. That will be the male.' So that night the man crept down to the sitting-room and after a short time he saw the two budgies 'on the job'. He quickly put his hand into the cage, grabbed the top bird and tied a piece of white cotton round its neck. The next morning the vicar called and was asked to wait in the sitting-room. The male budgie spotted the vicar's white dog collar and called out: 'Oh, so he caught you at it too, did he?' . . .

Seventh Over # The sun shines sweetly on cricket 1976

The year 1975 had been hailed as the golden summer, with its glorious weather and champagne cricket provided by the World Cup, and the Australian tour. However, 1976 did even better. The series against West Indies inspired brilliant stroke-play and devastating fast bowling, which those lucky enough to see will never forget. As for the sunshine, the weather beat all records, and needless to say that indispensable Bible of Cricket *Wisden* gave us all the details. A spell of fifteen days in June/July was the hottest and longest over the previous two hundred and fifty years. Up to the end of August there was the driest sixteen-month period since records for England and Wales began in 1727. Whew! It makes one sweat just to think of it. But the cricketers revelled in it and cricket itself prospered as a result. There were record crowds and receipts and increased sponsorship and membership. Over £1,000,000 was distributed among the counties at the end of the season.

The four main competitions were fiercely and closely contested. Middlesex brought the Championship back to Lord's for the first time since 1949, and Kent, acknowledged masters of the limited-over game, won both the Benson and Hedges and John Player trophies – the latter by the narrowest possible margin. In fact the result was in doubt until Glamorgan had bowled the very last ball to Somerset at Cardiff on the final day of the season. Off this ball, Somerset, 188 for 8, needed 3 to tie and 4 to win the match but a tie would have been sufficient for them to win the trophy. But they could only manage 2, Dredge being run out when going for the third, which would have meant Somerset winning their first-ever competition.

What a finish, and as a result Kent with the same number of points and away wins as Essex, won the John Player by 0.42 of a run on the faster scoring rate throughout the season. You can't have it much closer than that, and poor Essex too were robbed of what would have been their first-ever win of any of the four competitions.

With finishes such as these it is easy to understand the current popularity of limited-over cricket. One of its best points is that it distributes the honours round the seventeen counties, some of whom would never have a chance of winning the County Championship. This is still the real test of which is the best county, though it's not an ideal one. First of all each county only plays twenty-two matches which means that they all play each other at least once, but only six of the counties *twice*. Some counties too, like Kent, may have to supply three or even four of their top players for five Tests and three one-day Prudential matches so that players like Knott and Underwood play only ten or so out of the twenty-two County Championship games, plus missing five or so John Player matches. I know that Yorkshire used to supply up to five players regularly for England and still ran away with the Championship year after year. But at that time Tests only lasted for three or four days. In addition the other counties had not signed up star overseas players which today means that all the counties are far more evenly matched. Up to the middle fifties there were only the 'big six' who regularly dominated the Championship, and counties like Yorkshire and Surrey during their long run of successes would reckon to win many of their matches against the weaker brethren in two days. But to prove the point that the honours are now more evenly distributed Northants won the Gillette Cup Final at Lord's, so leaving only Essex and Somerset non-winners of any event.

In the 1976 Test Matches England were outclassed and the West Indies won the Wisden Trophy 3–0. Their batting line-up was possibly the strongest I have ever seen in Test cricket and they were all magnificent stroke-players – not a dawdler among them. Just look at this for a batting order: Fredericks, Greenidge, Richards, Kallicharran, Lloyd, King or Rowe. And to support them a terrifying trio of fast bowlers

Roberts, Holding, Daniel, plus Holder for good measure. It's not surprising that this was the most successful West Indies team ever to tour England winning eighteen of their twenty-six first-class matches, including three Tests, plus all three of the Prudential Trophy matches.

England could do little to counter this great side except to bring back Brian Close in his forty-fifth year, knowing that he would present a valiant and immovable target for the West Indian bouncers. These they bowled to excess in England's first innings at Old Trafford. It made a travesty of experimental Law 46, Note 4, VI, that the two umpires did not intervene as bouncer followed bouncer, until finally Bill Alley did warn Holding after he had bowled *three in succession* to Close. The combined ages of Edrich and Close was eighty-four and their batting on the Saturday evening was the bravest I have ever seen. But what a pity that Clive Lloyd, a nice gentle character, allowed the bombardment to take place.

The First Test at Trent Bridge was drawn and from the start England's tactics showed that that was all they were hoping to achieve. After losing the toss Greig set a purely defensive field and on several occasions had there been more close fielders the West Indies batsmen might well have been caught. As it was Viv Richards played a superb innings of 232 with four 6's and thirty-one 4's, many of them sizzling drives which left the fielders standing. He and Kallicharran put on 303 for the third wicket, but one felt that Greig's tactics were at fault. He bowled Hendrick – always susceptible to injury – unchanged for two hours, but Underwood who finished with 4–82 was not brought on to bowl until 5.45 pm when the total was 235. Strange use of the greatest left-arm bowler in the world.

In reply to West Indies' 494, England batted inconsistently for 332, Steele continuing from where he left off in 1975 with a typical fighting 106 – his first Test hundred. He was well supported by Woolmer (82), Old (33) and Snow (20) but single figures from Close, Brearley, Greig and Knott showed up the fragility of the England batting. When West Indies batted again, Snow – given a more attacking field – bowled with all his old life and took four wickets.

Richards (63) again played well and West Indies declared at 11.35 am on the fifth day, setting England to get 339 to win in five and a quarter hours – a target they were never likely to try for. They finished up with 156 for 2, Edrich (76) and Close (36) making sure that there was no panic after Brearley and Steele had gone cheaply.

During the West Indies' second innings there was one rather interesting point of law. Greenidge was lame and King – *who was not playing in the match* – was sent out as a runner, to which England, rightly to my mind, objected. Admittedly there is nothing in the laws to say who can or who can not come on as a runner. All Law 2 says is 'Substitutes shall be allowed to field or run between the wickets for any player who may during the match be incapacitated by illness or injury, but not for any other reason without the consent of the opposing captain; no substitute shall be allowed to bat or bowl. Consent as to the person to act as a substitute on the field shall be obtained from the opposing captain, who may indicate positions in which the substitute shall not field.'

Two points here:

1. In this country at least – and I must admit I thought in every other cricketing country – it is the custom that a runner should be someone playing in the batting eleven, and preferably someone who has already batted. A runner who has still to go in gets an advantage by being out in the middle for some time before having to bat. He gets a sight of the ball, and advance knowledge of the bowlers and pace of the wicket.

But the West Indies' manager, Clyde Walcott, protested when the umpires upheld the English objection, saying that so far as he was concerned *anyone* could act as runner. This conjures up all sorts of possibilities with professional sprinters being specially employed to stand by all padded up, to be sent out to race up and down the wicket.

2. The words 'during the match' in Law 2 are important and recall the 'Kanhai incident' during Peter May's tour of the West Indies in 1959–60. Kanhai had gone into the match with a dodgy knee and during his second innings of 57 asked if he could have a runner. Peter May refused, and this

caused quite a furore at the time. But all ended happily with
Peter apologising when he learnt that it was cramp at the
back of the leg, and not his knee which had been troubling
Kanhai. But the incident did remind people that a player
should not ask for a substitute because of an aggravation of
an injury which he had at the start of the match. But since
the Law specifically states that permission need only be
sought of the fielding captain for something *other than* illness
or injury, presumably a decision about them is in the hands
of the umpires.

So England got away with the draw they wanted at Trent
Bridge, but at Lord's their defensive outlook probably rob-
bed them of a win. After winning the toss they took all of the
first day to score 197 for 8, though admittedly the West
Indies only bowled just over eighty overs. It took
Underwood the next morning with a slog of 31 to raise
England's total to 250. It was to be his day because this time
Greig had learnt his lesson and brought him on early. He
bowled superbly taking 5 for 39 backed up by a fiery Snow (4
for 68) and West Indies were all out for 182 – 68 runs behind.
Saturday alas was rained off completely with a full crowd
inside the ground and thousands locked outside the gates.

But on Monday England failed to push the score along.
Admittedly, Wood had retired hurt with a damaged finger
and Pocock the nightwatchman and Brearley were out. But
Steele (64) and Close (46) in a stand of 83 allowed the
comparatively innocuous slow left-arm bowler Jumadeen to
bowl nine overs for only 16 runs. England made 254 and so
West Indies needed 323 in just over five hours. They finished
up with 241 for 6, the match going to the last of the statutory
twenty overs, with only Murray and the tail-enders between
England and victory. One couldn't help feeling that had they
scored more quickly on Monday, and so given themselves
more time to bowl West Indies out, England might have
snatched an unlikely victory. At any rate it was to be their
last chance of doing so in the series.

At Old Trafford England were annihilated by some of the
fastest and most dangerous bowling I have ever seen. For
some reason the pitch was full of cracks and as a result was
two-paced and with a variable bounce. England did well to

bowl out West Indies for only 211, out of which Greenidge made a beautiful 134. Selvey in his first Test swung the ball and took 4–41. But when England batted only Steele (20) reached double figures, though extras thanks to eleven no balls contributed 19. Roberts (3–22) Holding (5–17) and Daniel (2–13) were devastating and against such frightening speed with the ball lifting unpredictably one found it hard to blame the England batsmen who were all out for 71.

West Indies went to town in their second innings with Greenidge (101) making his second hundred of the match and Richards, who couldn't play at Lord's, following up his 232 and 63 at Trent Bridge with a fine 135.

England had to bat again for eighty minutes on Saturday night and it was then that the West Indian fast bowlers seemed to go mad. They hurled bouncers indiscriminately at Edrich and Close, who resisted with tremendous bravery and somehow avoided serious injury. There was uproar in the Press over the weekend and I hope we on radio and TV spoke out against it as strongly as it deserved. Anyhow, on the Monday, although still bowling very fast, the bowlers pitched the ball up on a length and with Roberts taking 6 for 37 England were all out for 126 and so were beaten by 425 runs. A moral here surely. Good bowling will always take more wickets than the loathsome short-pitched stuff, which is not only dangerous but ruins cricket as a spectacle.

Although England lost the Fourth Test at Headingley by 55 runs – and with it the series and the Wisden Trophy – they fought back magnificently after a disastrous first day. Even in Bradman's time Headingley can never have seen so many brilliant strokes as were played by Fredericks and Greenidge. They both made hundreds putting on 192 for the first wicket, with Greenidge scoring his third hundred in succession. Nothing could stop them and at lunch West Indies were 147–0 off only twenty-seven overs – a scoring rate of over $5\frac{1}{2}$ runs per over on the first day of a Test Match! At close of play, from 330 for 2 at tea, they 'collapsed' to 437 for 9 off only eighty-three overs. So in spite of losing seven wickets after tea when the ball surprisingly began to swing and seam, West Indies kept up a scoring rate of over 5 runs per over.

It was tremendous batting with Richards chipping in with another fine innings of 66. But credit is also due to the three England pace bowlers – Snow (4–77), Willis (3–71) and Ward (2–103), who in spite of the initial onslaught never gave up.

With West Indies all out for 450 England made their usual poor start and were soon 32 for 3. But thanks to Balderstone (35), Willey (36) and a great stand of 152 between Greig and Knott who both made 116, England reached the respectable total of 387, only 63 runs behind. They then went on to confirm what an unpredictable game cricket is, by bowling out West Indies for only 196, thanks to some superb fast bowling by Willis with 5–42. This meant that England had the perfectly possible task of scoring 260 to win in roughly a day and a half. But once again the pendulum swung and England were soon 23–3. But Woolmer (37), Willey (45) and Greig (76) attacked the bowling and had anyone been able to stay with Greig, England might just have snatched a sensational victory. But the last six wickets fell for 64 runs and they were all out for 204, the three batsmen named being the only ones to reach double figures. But though they lost the match England had shown that given the right conditions to produce swing and seam, the brilliant West Indian stroke-makers could be contained and bowled out. The three successful England batsmen also showed that aggression against the battery of fast bowlers paid off better than defence.

The return of Alan Ward to the Test scene after an absence of fifty-one Tests revived the old story of how he had once gone on a club tour of Germany during which he had taken a hat-trick against a team of Germans. From then on he was known as Jerryatric Ward!

West Indies' easy victory at the Oval by the huge margin of 231 runs after declaring twice, merely emphasised what a great side they were. It also made it all the more difficult to understand how they themselves had succumbed so easily to Australia during the previous winter. Was the partnership of Lillee and Thomson on their own bouncy pitches practically unplayable? I myself suspect that it was, and that not too much blame can be attached to either Mike Denness' or Clive Lloyd's batsmen.

Anyway, at the Oval all the West Indies' batsmen prospered. Richards (291) with another superb double century was supported by all the batsmen except Greenidge and in their first innings of 687 for 8 declared there were no fewer than five innings of over 60. The incredible Richards, until tiredness overtook him, looked as if nothing could stop him beating Sobers' record Test score of 365. He finished the series with the fantastic average of 118.42 for his 829 runs. On his form of this summer he must be toppling Barry Richards off the throne of No. 1 batsman in the world. Viv has had an amazingly quick rise to the top, but I'm sure that Barry is only in danger of losing his crown because of the lack of opportunity and incentive he has had in not playing in Tests against top-class opposition.

England's reply of 435 was based on an innings of great guts and character by Dennis Amiss on his return to Test cricket. After the terrible battering he had received from Lillee and Thomson in Australia – he had four innings of 4, 5, 0, 10 against them in England in 1975, he was dropped after the Second Test. Instead of throwing in the sponge he took advantage of his absence to work out a new technique against fast bowlers. Basically it consisted of shuffling across to the off-stump or even just outside *before the bowler delivered the ball*. It looked ugly and dangerous, too, because he was nearly square on when he received the ball and so was still in trouble to any ball which left him late outside the offstump. But at least he was behind the line of the ball, though his leg stump was temptingly exposed to the bowler.

The first time he tried it out against Roberts and Holding was for MCC at Lord's when he failed in both innings (9 and 11). What was more he was struck on the back of the head turning his back on a short ball from Holding. He pluckily came back with four stitches in his head but it really did look as if his Test career was over – at least against any country with fast bowlers. I must say in his defence that I sat sideways on to the pitch on the Saturday evening of the MCC match and I have never seen faster bowling than that of Holding. A thrilling sight for the spectator with the added bonus of a flowing and balanced run-up, his feet seeming scarcely to touch the ground as he sprinted like a gazelle to deliver the ball.

Anyway after four Tests England were still unable to find a satisfactory opening partnership, the opening stands being 0, 38, 15, 29, 9, 54, 4, 5. So the selectors decided to gamble on the class which Amiss undoubtedly has and he rewarded them by making his return a dramatic success. He scored 203 out of 342 in five hours twenty minutes, hitting twenty-eight 4's. A great tribute to the determination of this nice, solid, pipe-smoking character. But to bear out what I said earlier, he was finally bowled *behind his legs*.

Although West Indies were 252 runs on Lloyd did not enforce the follow-on and once again the West Indies' batsmen showed their complete mastery of the England bowling, Fredericks (86) and Greenidge (85) putting on 182 for the first wicket before Lloyd declared, leaving England 435 to win – their total in the first innings. Needless to say they found this an impossible task against some more magnificent fast bowling by Holding, who finished the match with fourteen wickets, both he and Roberts getting twenty-eight apiece in the series. Steele made his second 40 of the match and Knott his second 50 but England were all out for 203.

So the West Indies won the series 3–0 and must rival the 1950 side as the best ever to tour England from West Indies. All they lacked from a point of view of balance was a class off-spinner or slow left-arm bowler. But with their wonderful array of fast bowlers it is doubtful whether such a spinner – however good – would have got more than a few overs in any of the Tests.

It may be many years before we shall see again such a superb combination of brilliant stroke makers and lightning fast bowlers. It may also be many years before we enjoy another such hot, dry summer, which of course was just what the doctor ordered for the particular talents of this West Indian side. As for England, they were simply beaten by a far better side in the conditions. And yet under Greig's captaincy there were new signs of a developing team spirit and an ability to fight back. But until the new generation of promising young batsmen developed it looked as if the batting would be the main problem in the immediate future.

One amusing incident occurred during the West Indies second innings. For many years now I have written short articles for the benefit brochures of players. I have naturally done it for nothing as part of my contribution to their well-deserved benefit – that is all except once. When Alan Knott had his benefit he asked me as usual to write something for him. I replied that I would be delighted but for the first time ever I was going to charge him for my work. This shook him a bit but he bravely asked me what my fee would be. I told him that my payment would be a promise from him that, if Bob Woolmer played in a Test during the summer, he would stand up to the stumps for at least one over.

This business of standing up happens to be a hobby horse of mine, since the days when Godfrey Evans stood up to Alec Bedser and kept so brilliantly. Nowadays all Test wicket-keepers stand back to every bowler other than the all too rare spinners. Farooq Engineer was an honourable exception. I think Gil Langley probably started it when he began standing back to the medium pace of Ken Mackay. Even that superb wicket-keeper Wally Grout did so too, encouraged I believe by his captain Richie Benaud.

Jim Parks stood back to Basil D'Oliveira and so did Knotty. Also when keeping for Kent he stood back to Shepherd, Asif and Woolmer. I've had a friendly running argument about it with him for years: he maintains that if he stands up he runs the risk of dropping a vital catch, and that it is not worth it for the few stumpings which might result. He and others also claim that they might unsight the leg slip who is placed there to take the sort of catch on the leg side which a wicket-keeper standing up would try for. This is possible. But I wonder whether you have noticed that with the restriction of only two men allowed behind the popping crease on the leg side, a leg slip is becoming rarer and rarer. Anyway, I feel that such a brilliant wicket-keeper as Knotty would be very unlikely to miss a chance, however difficult, and that the benefits of standing up far outweigh the risks.

First of all it exerts pressure on the batsman. With some-one breathing down his neck he has something extra to think about. He dare not risk taking up his stance a foot or so in front of the popping crease as some batsmen do to the fast medium bowler bowling just short of a length. He has to remember to keep his back foot behind the line, and if he misses the ball must not overbalance. Next it gives the bowler a target to aim at. Alec Bedser always asked his wicket-keepers to stand up, and pays tribute to 'Godders' and that much underrated wicket-keeper Arthur McIntyre for the great help they were to him. It also makes a medium or fast medium bowler look far more penetrating and aggressive when the ball goes with a thud into the wicket-keeper's hands close to the stumps. Nothing depreciates a bowler more than a ball landing with a gentle 'plop' into the gloves of a wicket-keeper standing right back.

And finally but most important these days is the increase in entertainment value of a brilliant take or stumping on the leg side by a wicket-keeper standing up. It's all very well seeing the modern-day wicket-keepers flinging themselves all over the place like goalkeepers. It's certainly athletic and results in some remarkable catches, usually one-handed, but which might in fact have been caught by one of the slips anyway. I was talking to Les Ames at Canterbury and told him that I never remembered seeing *him* hurling himself about. In fact my impression was that he always seemed to get across behind the line of the ball and stay on his feet – and the same went for Bertie Oldfield too. Les admitted that he had never flung himself to the ground and added that it was considered 'undignified' for a wicket-keeper to fall over in those days! Maybe he didn't consider as chances those wide balls at which wicket-keepers fling themselves today. I wonder!

But back to Knotty and the payment of my fee. When Bob Woolmer came on to bowl in the West Indies' second innings, Knotty turned round to the commentary box, gave me the thumbs-up and went right up to the stumps. And of course it *would* happen. Bob's first ball was a near wide outside the leg stump of left-hander Roy Fredericks. Knotty only just managed to get a right hand to it, so saving four certain byes. He turned round and gave me a 'there you are I told you so' sort of look. But he gallantly stood up for two overs and made some brilliant takes. I am sure that if he were to stand up more often he would prove that he is possibly the greatest wicket-keeper ever. It is only the lack of proof that he *can* match Evans' brilliant keeping when standing up to the quicker bowls that leaves a question mark.

By the way my TV colleagues were not in the know about what was going on, and were speculating that Knott and Woolmer were plotting some trap like a leg-side stumping. Incidents like this surely prove that even in Test cricket there is room for a bit of fun.

During the summer, 1976, I was lucky enough to be asked to commentate on one of the three Women's Test Matches in the series against Australia. It was the Golden Jubilee of the Women's Cricket Association and though the three Tests were all drawn, England won the limited-over one-day matches 2–1. Furthermore, their jubilee was celebrated by a unique and memorable occasion. The second of these matches was played at Lord's on a pitch in the centre of the ground, on a flawless day before a remarkably large and enthusiastic crowd. So after much propaganda, lobbying and arm-twisting the ladies had at last been allowed to enter the Holy of Holies even to the extent of using the dressing-rooms and baths, hitherto exclusive male preserves. So far as I was concerned as a member of MCC it was a most welcome invasion. Everyone present at Lord's on that day was, I'm sure, grateful to the good sense of MCC, and to the enthusiastic, untiring and witty vocal efforts of England's captain, Rachel Heyhoe-Flint, which had brought it all about.

I am seldom so presumptuous as to disagree with an opinion expressed by a revered England cricket captain, but I did so once. The occasion was a match on Chislehurst Green between Colin Cowdrey's XI and the Women's England XI of that time. I was keeping wicket and Len Hutton was at first slip. So I asked him what he thought of women playing cricket. He gave me a funny look and answered: 'It's just like a man trying to knit, isn't it?' But as I've said I disagreed – and incidentally the women won the match. In fact I have always supported the girls, and think that they've got quite a bit to teach us men. First-class cricket nowadays tends to be rather scientific or 'professional ' as it's so often called. The ladies bring a touch of grace into what is essentially a graceful game. Anyone who has watched women play recently will know that as bats*men* they use their feet to the slow bowlers. They have all the strokes and run like hinds between the wickets. In the old days if you wished to insult a fielder you told him that he threw like a girl. Nowadays their returns from the outfield come whistling back over the top of the stumps. Their fielding is remarkably keen and their bowling subtle and steady, though lacking in pace.

I have played quite a bit of cricket with women. At my private school the headmaster's daughter, Kitten, bowled a nifty leg-break and in the holidays we used to play a mixed match in the village of Much Marcle in Herefordshire. The star was a retired bishop's wife called Mrs Whitehead. She was a left-hander and defended dourly, and usually carried her bat. In later years I saw her exact replica in Test cricket – Slasher Mackay, the impassive Australian – though Mrs Whitehead did not chew gum!

Mothers, too, have played an important part in cricket. Perhaps the best example, as I've mentioned before, was in Australia where Vic Richardson's daughter, Mrs Chappell, coached her three sons, Ian, Greg and Trevor in the back garden with results which we in England know all too well. Penny Cowdrey, too, is another mother brought up on garden cricket, where for years her bowling tested her three sons, Christopher, Jeremy and Graham. Even more important to me personally was the fact that early in our courtship I discovered that my wife Pauline could throw a cricket ball really well. I won't pretend that it was a vital factor in our romance, but it helped!

I hope by now it is obvious that I am one hundred per cent in favour of women's cricket, and wish them success in the years ahead, though unlike the lady jockeys they will never be strong enough to compete on equal terms with men.

There is one small change which I would like to see. I wish they would wear trousers instead of those divided skirts. I'm always worried that the pad straps will chafe the back of their knees. I also think they deserve to get more coverage on radio and TV, though I can see one or two pitfalls for commentators. What girl would enjoy hearing that she had two short legs? On the other hand I suppose none of them would object if they heard that they had a very fine long leg. And finally, since they bring such glamour and a sense of chivalry and good manners into the game, isn't it about time they were called Ladies instead of Women?

Eighth Over Captains courageous

During my thirty-two years of broadcasting cricket, the England selectors have appointed thirteen captains for Test series in this country. In addition, Nigel Howard and Tony Lewis captained England in India only, and Ken Cranston, David Sheppard, Tom Graveney and John Edrich took over as substitute captains *during* a Test Series. I have, with one exception, been lucky enough to know them all well, either from travelling with them on tour, or from commentary and interviews. The one exception was Wally Hammond, whom strangely enough I never met until 1965 in South Africa when he was 'adopted' by Mike Smith's team and made a tremendous fuss of. This was particularly nice to see as his life in the post-war years had been sad. Anyway, for some reason, in 1946, although we televised the Lord's and Oval Tests against India, there were no interviews with the captains. So although I saw him as captain in two Tests and Lewis and Howard as captains of Glamorgan and Lancashire I cannot really claim to know at first hand their qualities as Test captains.

I am often asked who was the best Test captain of all those whom I did know, and it's an almost impossible question to answer. Each one has so many different qualities – some good, some not so good. So before trying to give an answer I think it would be helpful to give a pen picture of each one, and to analyse their strengths and weaknesses. So to start with, here are the qualities which I think are essential for the ideal captain to have, and it all adds up to an awful lot of 'musts'.

He must:
1. Be a leader whose team will respect and follow him.

2. Be absolutely fair with no favourites, and get to know each member of his team – not just the stars. He will then be able to understand their moods and problems. Cricketers are not automatons, and the good captain is one who knows when to reprimand, encourage or sympathise.

3. Know all the laws of cricket and all the many regulations which seem to get more complicated every year.

4. Be a good enough player to be in the side on playing merit alone. It makes his job so much easier.

5. Be a good tactician and study the strengths and weaknesses of his opponents. Also be prepared to listen to the advice of his senior players and judge when to act on it.

6. Be able and prepared to deal with the broadcasters and the Press and to answer their questions clearly and honestly however stupid, critical or controversial they may be, or however inconvenient the time. They all have a job to do, and a happy Press who have confidence in the captain will mean that the activities of the team are reported in the best possible light.

7. Be a reasonable speaker – to be a *good* one is a bonus.

8. Off the field be a good mixer and expect to have to suffer fools gladly.

9. Take risks to win – that is the object of the game. But when to win is impossible then ensure that the team fights to the bitter end, to draw the game. Furthermore, make sure that each member of the team knows what the tactics are, and what part he is expected to play. Far too many Test captains give no instructions to their players, saying that if they are good enough to play in a Test, they should know what to do. This is a lot of codswallop and a complete dereliction of captaincy.

10. Instruct their players to 'play the game', i.e. no gamesmanship, frivolous appeals, swearing at opponents or obvious dissent with the umpire's decision. This 'must' may well prove to be the most difficult of all to carry out!

11. Finally be LUCKY – perhaps the most essential quality of all.

Now let's see how the various captains pass on examination in all these 'musts'.

NORMAN YARDLEY

CHARACTER	LEADERSHIP	TACTICAL SKILL	PLAYING ABILITY	PR WITH MEDIA	OFF THE FIELD
Nice guy. Everyone's friend.	Too tolerant. Not tough enough.	Good and willing to take advice from senior pros. Did well v. South Africa in 1947 but was on a hiding to nothing v. Don Bradman's team of 1948 – arguably the best ever sent by Australia to England.	A schoolboy prodigy who came good. Very strong on leg side. Good field and a more than useful medium pace change bowler who got Bradman three times in Australia 1946–7.	Friendly and cooperative but did not have to cope with the pressure of TV nor the more modern down-to-earth interviews.	Never captained a touring team except when he took over from Hammond in Fifth Test in 1947. But would have been a perfect ambassador.

GEORGE MANN

CHARACTER	LEADERSHIP	TACTICAL SKILL	PLAYING ABILITY	PR WITH MEDIA	OFF THE FIELD
Product of Eton and the Guards with all their virtues and none of their vices. Friendly, straight and honest with strong principles.	A natural, undoubtedly helped by his distinguished leadership during the war with the Scots Guards.	Simple and basic, but always prepared to listen to his senior players and to take their advice.	A magnificent fielder who set a high standard. His batting not quite Test class. But for his character, would not have been worth his place.	Friendly and helpful but never under any real pressure.	Excellent. Very good mixer.

FREDDIE BROWN

CHARACTER	LEADERSHIP	TACTICAL SKILL	PLAYING ABILITY	PR WITH MEDIA	OFF THE FIELD
Bluff, blunt hale and hearty. A John Bull image!	Led by example. Lots of guts. Never gave up. Could express his wishes quite forcibly!	Sound. Based on many years of first-class cricket before and after the war. Prepared to take risks but on his Australian tour of 1950–1 never had the ammunition.	Originally a top class leg-spinner but in Australia in 1950–1 got most of his 18 test wickets with seamers. A hard-hitting batsman and a good fielder though not in the greyhound class.	Apt to be a bit impatient and suspicious (probably rightly) of certain sections of the Press. But generally friendly and informative.	Hale fellow well met but could be drawn into a fairly heated argument in which his opponent would be stabbed in the chest by a gigantic forefinger.

LEN HUTTON

CHARACTER	LEADERSHIP	TACTICAL SKILL	PLAYING ABILITY	PR WITH MEDIA	OFF THE FIELD
First of the professional captains. Reserved, withdrawn and wary with a dry wit and a twinkle in the eye. Appeared slightly suspicious of everyone and everything.	Not a natural but gained respect because of his great playing skill. Outwardly calm, but inwardly felt the pressures and got easily depressed. In the end it all got too much for him – hence his early retirement.	Mainly defensive but canny and well thought out. A good judge of the game and of his opponents' strengths and weaknesses. The first captain to introduce the slow over rate as a tactic. After the battering he himself had received from Lindwall and Miller he played the game hard and knew that NO ONE likes fast bowling – hence his great faith in Tyson.	A batsman of the highest possible class and a candidate for almost anyone's World XI of all time. Of all his many strokes the cover drive was the one I savour most.	Suspicious and reserved and could give answers in double talk which not only puzzled the interviewer but possibly Len himself!	Kept to himself but did the minimum required of a captain on the social side. Not a great speaker.

PETER MAY

CHARACTER	LEADERSHIP	TACTICAL SKILL	PLAYING ABILITY	PR WITH MEDIA	OFF THE FIELD
Friendly and pleasant with a certain schoolboy charm, but undoubtedly tough under the surface.	Unobtrusive but firm and expected anyone chosen to play in a Test to know what to do without being told. Played the game hard and relied on others to do the same. Preferred the grafter to the 'fancy' stroke player.	Followed in the Hutton tradition and like most Test captains preferred not to go for victory if it meant that there was the *slightest* risk of losing.	Top class – best batsman since the war. All the strokes but the on-drive his speciality. A sound fielder and a good close catcher.	Often felt he was unfairly treated hence tended to be suspicious and guarded in his answers. Difficult to get much out of him.	Socially very good and, although he didn't enjoy it, made an amusing speech with some gentle leg pulling.

COLIN COWDREY

CHARACTER	LEADERSHIP	TACTICAL SKILL	PLAYING ABILITY	PR WITH MEDIA	OFF THE FIELD
Gentle, friendly, good mannered, polite, sensitive. Tremendous enthusiasm for life, people and cricket, aided by his strong religious beliefs.	Established good team spirit and expected high standard of behaviour. Took great trouble to look after team off the field and to make sure they enjoyed the tour. On the field not dominant nor assertive enough when the crunch came.	Great knowledge of the individual techniques required, and had a deep knowledge of the game and all its traditions. Strangely defensive at times and asked *too* many people's advice which sometimes meant postponing vital decisions.	Outstanding, might have been the greatest of all but for strange lapses of confidence in his own ability. Magnificent timer of the ball with every stroke in the book plus 'the paddle' down to fine leg. A brilliant slip-fielder – one of the best ever.	Excellent. Took infinite trouble to try to help and made a point of involving the media on the tour with his team.	Certainly the best I have seen. Nothing too much trouble – infinite patience with everyone and attended every social function: visited schools, hospitals, churches, etc. A very good speaker.

TED DEXTER

CHARACTER	LEADERSHIP	TACTICAL SKILL	PLAYING ABILITY	PR WITH MEDIA	OFF THE FIELD
Could be haughty and aloof – could be the friendliest of persons. A man of moods. Nickname of 'Lord Edward' gives a good picture of his superb bearing and physique with the suspicion of him being slightly above mere mortals.	Largely by example when either batting or fielding. A great gambler in everyday life this was not reflected in his leadership which tended to be defensive.	Too much theory mingled with pragmatic inspiration or ideas. Not always easy to follow his line of thought!	Magnificent attacking player at his best when 'seeing off' fast bowlers with brilliant strokes off the front or back foot, especially the latter. A more than useful medium fast change bowler who would have been better handled by someone else!	Tried to cooperate but one got the impression that the media was something to be tolerated with the job.	Dependent on his moods. Could be excellent and always a great party-goer.

MIKE SMITH

CHARACTER	LEADERSHIP	TACTICAL SKILL	PLAYING ABILITY	PR WITH MEDIA	OFF THE FIELD
The players' captain. Unflappable, quiet, dry wit, great debunker of conceit and pomposity. A leg-puller whose somewhat 'owlish' appearance hid a good sense of humour.	Unobtrusive. Never asked anyone to do anything he would not do himself. Chose to field in the most dangerous close positions, and to take the batting risks himself when necessary. Not afraid to go for victory, but once a lead in a series had been achieved he was apt to 'sit on it'.	Sound with a good knowledge of the game but with an instinct against using spinners, possibly because he played them so well himself. Good at pressurising new batsmen.	Not quite consistent enough to rate in the top Test class. Vulnerable against fast bowling early in his innings. Especially strong on the leg side and developed 'the lap'. A good runner between the wickets and a superb fielder at short leg in spite of his glasses.	Pretty cagey and could act dumb under pressure of questioning. Difficult to get much out of him, though he was always friendly and cooperative.	Very good at the cricketer level but not too keen on the more formal social occasions and receptions, though he tried hard!

BRIAN CLOSE

CHARACTER	LEADERSHIP	TACTICAL SKILL	PLAYING ABILITY	PR WITH MEDIA	OFF THE FIELD
Brave, tough, gutsy, determined, obstinate with a delightful sense of humour and an unexpected giggle. Great talker – on any subject.	Strong leader who didn't mince his words. Highly respected by his players. Never gave up and encouraged his team to fight to the bitter end. He always made sure everyone knew what was expected of them.	More adventurous than most and full of Yorkshire cunning. A great believer in pressurising the opposition at every opportunity.	Never really reached his true potential. A natural games player. Tremendous guts standing up to fast bowling. Was discarded by selectors too early in his career. Fine close fielder standing suicidally within reach of the bat. A useful off-spin change bowler.	Very good and prepared to answer most questions in a down to earth though somewhat lengthy manner!	Good – especially if the other person or persons were prepared to listen!

RAY ILLINGWORTH

CHARACTER	LEADERSHIP	TACTICAL SKILL	PLAYING ABILITY	PR WITH MEDIA	OFF THE FIELD
Typical Yorkshireman with slight chip on shoulder and suspicious of most Southerners and the establishment of cricket. Dry sense of humour and good business sense.	Another players' captain who looked after his men both on and off the field. Got to know their problems and their moods. Knew when to encourage or sympathise. Fought for their welfare in every way. *On the field* his expertise gained their 100 per cent support.	The best tactician of all. Great understanding of the game and an unrivalled assessor of his opponents' strengths and weaknesses. A good 'reader' of a match.	Made himself into a Test all-rounder and performed many rescue acts for England batting at No. 7. Tended to underbowl himself unless conditions were ideal for his off-spin with its variation of flight and pace. A useful gully.	One of the best captains whom I ever interviewed. Never shirked a question. However awkward it was, one got a straight answer – too straight for some!	The social niceties of a tour came bottom on his list of priorities. But he enjoyed a party.

MIKE DENNESS

CHARACTER	LEADERSHIP	TACTICAL SKILL	PLAYING ABILITY	PR WITH MEDIA	OFF THE FIELD
A friendly, chirpy but determined Scot with a cheerful outlook on life. Could be obstinate. Never as popular with his own Kent side as with other people. This may possibly have been partly due to his method of team selection.	At the start of his Test captaincy was apt to be too much of a loner, and did not consult his senior players. Was in a difficult position with five or six of his side having played in far more Tests than himself. Later when he had proved himself he did take advice but after that fateful 'team' decision to put Australia in at Edgbaston, probably now wishes he hadn't.	Shrewd enough, and perfected the tactics for limited-over cricket. Strangely, often seemed not to make the best use of Underwood.	A fine player of spin but on Australian tour showed a weakness of technique against Lillee and Thomson – but he was not the *only* one! An unselfish batsman who was prepared to take risks to make up for a slow start. A magnificent fielder especially in the covers.	Friendly enough but could show a certain amount of Scottish canniness when facing a difficult question.	A good mixer and useful speaker.

CHARACTER	LEADERSHIP	TACTICAL SKILL	PLAYING ABILITY	PR WITH MEDIA	OFF THE FIELD
Blond, tall, glamorous, good looking and friendly with lots of charm. Becomes a grimmer character on the field with a fierce determination to win, though still retaining his showmanship and outsize personality so far as the crowds are concerned.	A superb leader who created tremendous team spirit on a tour. Believed in involving his *whole* team, not just those playing in the Tests. Succeeded in imparting to them his own will to win or at least to fight 100 per cent. Believed in pressurising opposing batsmen by aggressive field placing, but more questionably seemed to believe in occasional pressure by *talking* to batsmen.	The weakest part of his captaincy though he improved slightly in India. Strangely defensive for such a character. Seemed to want to establish an unassailable base before taking risks to win. Some of his bowling changes and field placings against West Indies in 1976 made even me speechless!	A fine attacking batsman, but lacking in consistency. Helped by his long reach which makes bowling to him difficult. Magnificent at driving the ball or forcing it off the back foot. His habit of holding his bat aloft 'at the ready' makes his leg stump very vulnerable to a fast yorker. A magnificent fielder anywhere and one of the finest slip catchers I have ever seen. His fast medium bowling inconsistent but always liable to take a wicket when brought on to break a stand. His off-spin too unreliable to be effective.	The best ever in answering every question as truthfully and as candidly as possible. Nothing ever too much trouble for him but in his efforts to help the interviewer and give good value sometimes overdid it – eg his 'We'll make them grovel' remark about the West Indies.	First-class rapport with everyone and always seemed to do the right thing. Created tremendous charisma by his charm and glamorous appearance.

MIKE BREARLEY

CHARACTER	LEADERSHIP	TACTICAL SKILL	PLAYING ABILITY	PR WITH MEDIA	OFF THE FIELD
Outwardly a quiet, compassionate, friendly person with a nice smile, a good sense of humour and a strong social conscience. Inside a far tougher character with strong opinions and plenty of determination. Highly intelligent he got a first at Cambridge and passed top in the Civil Service exam. Always sympathetic to the underdog, and although I don't think he is really anti-establishment he is by inclination on the side of the workers!	Quiet and unobtrusive but firm. Never raises his voice. Asks for, and takes, advice from his senior players. Inherited the team spirit originally created by Greig, but has maintained and fostered it. Genuinely liked by the players. Made a great start by winning back the Ashes in his first series as captain.	A great student of of the game. Gives it much deep thought, especially field placing. Has a happy knack of timing his bowling changes correctly.	To me he is not quite Test class but will always produce a sound innings with some stylish strokes. Nurtured on the splendid Fenner pitches when he was at Cambridge. Plenty of guts and never flinches at the fast bowlers, possibly given confidence by his plastic skull protector. Originally a wicket-keeper is now a highly competent catcher at first slip.	Absolutely first-class. Cooperative, friendly and happy to answer any reasonable question. Takes any implied criticism in good part.	Unfortunately I have never been on a tour with him. But with his basic friendly and sympathetic character I would expect him to be a great success.

And there you have my assessments of the thirteen Test captains. You may well have very different ideas as to their characters and ability. But these are *my* opinions and based on them I have chosen the one who I think has been the best *all round* captain. I will give my verdict and reasons right at the end of the book. So why don't you make *your* choice now and see whether we agree? If you want to crib, the answer is on page 220.

And as a final guide here is a table (accurate until end August 1977) showing the varying success of each captain.

| | No. of times Captain | MATCHES | | |
		Won	Lost	Drawn
Yardley	15	4	8	3
Mann	7	2	0	5
Brown	15	5	6	4
Hutton	20	9	3	8
May	41	21	10	10
Cowdrey	27	8	4	15
Dexter	30	9	7	14
Smith	25	5	3	17
Close	7	6	0	1
Illingworth	31	12	5	14
Denness	19	6	6	7
Greig	14	3	5	6
Brearley	5	3	0	2

Ninth Over Out of the mouths . . .

In *It's Been A Lot of Fun* I listed quite a few of my better known gaffes which I have made during cricket commentaries. Not only do they still happen but people keep reminding me of ones which I had forgotten all about. Such as when a few years ago a mouse ran across the pitch during a Test Match at Edgbaston. Play was held up while players tried to catch it, and the poor little mouse showed up beautifully on our TV zoom lens. I was doing the commentary on TV and when describing the chase said: 'They are bound to catch it soon – it's got no hole to go down.' I then unfortunately added: 'Lucky it's not a ladies' match.' All I meant was that they would be rushing about screaming as they are always meant to do when they see a mouse. But Denis Compton especially thought it was very funny!

There was also the occasion when I evidently greeted listeners with these words: 'You join us at an interesting time. Ray Illingworth has just relieved himself at the Pavilion End!'

After the Test Match at the Oval against the West Indies I received a letter which I suspect was a leg-pull, though I am not sure. I was suspicious because it was signed by a Miss Mainpiece! She begged me to be more careful what I said because so many young boys listened to our radio commentaries. She then cited an example of what she meant by accusing me of saying at the beginning of an over bowled by the West Indian fast bowler Michael Holding to Peter Willey – 'The bowler's Holding the batsman's Willey!' If I *did* say it I swear I didn't mean it!

I also made a completely nonsensical remark at Northampton during the August match between Northants and

Worcestershire. Although it could have had an important influence on the result of the County Championship there was a disappointingly small crowd there. And I said, 'There's a disappointing crowd here today, just a few cars scattered around the boundary boards. In fact' – I went on – 'I would say that there are more cars here today than people!' Just work that one out – did the cars drive themselves in?

But even the most innocent remark can have a double meaning – *if* you have that sort of mind! Such as when on one occasion I said to Radio 2 listeners who had just joined us: 'D'Oliveira is getting badly punished by the Hampshire batsmen. A moment or two before you joined us Barry Richards hit one of Dolly's balls clean out of the ground.' A perfectly innocent remark but one that produced sniggers in the commentary box as my companions conjured up visions of this remarkable and very painful feat!

But the cricket commentators are not the only ones who drop clangers, and the Olympic Games at Montreal produced one or two good ones. During the swimming Peter Jones on the radio said: 'It's the pool that sets the spectators alight', and Alan Weekes on TV: 'If Wilkie goes on like this he'll be home and dry!' It seems uncertain whether it was David Coleman or Ron Pickering who during the 800 metres final talking about Juantorena the eventual winner commented on TV: 'Every time the big Cuban opens his legs, he shows his class!'

Frank Bough has admitted he once said as he handed over to a boxing fight, '. . . and your carpenter is Harry Commentator'. One of the most famous, of course, was John Snagge's desperate cry during the Boat Race when his launch could not keep up with the boats. 'I don't know who's ahead – it's either Oxford or Cambridge!'

But it was the golf commentators who had the biggest nightmare of all, and nightly went down on their knees and prayed that Coles would not be drawn to play against Hunt.

Two more gaffes are attributed to David Coleman. The first at the Montreal Olympic Games where he said: 'To win a gold medal you've GOT to come first.' The second was at a League match in which Manchester United were playing:

'United are buzzing around the goalmouth like a lot of red blue-bottles.'

Another good soccer one came from John Motson during the 1977 FA Cup Final. 'If Liverpool lose today it will cast grave doubts on their ability to win the treble.'

But poor Hugh Johns made a perfectly innocent remark on ITV to which some dirty-minded (!) people took exception. All he said was, 'The referee is now looking at his whistle!'

Jimmy Hill is credited with this gem – 'Over now to Nigel Starmer-Smith who has had seven craps as scum-half for England!'

And there's a delightful one which Rex Alston made many years ago, '. . . So over now to Old John Arlott at Trafford.'

I am never quite certain who was the originator of *this* remark – not much double entendre about it! Anyway, it was a cricket commentator who was talking about Cunis the New Zealand fast bowler. 'Cunis,' he said, 'a funny sort of name. Neither one thing nor the other!' I promise you it wasn't me!

Incidentally, talking of names, Bill Frindall assures me that once when referring to Asif Mahsood the Pakistan bowler I called him by mistake: 'Masif *Ahsood*!'

And appropriately, in Jubilee Year, I was reminded recently of an occasion when Henry Riddell was the commentator on some royal procession or other. After describing the Queen's carriage and escorts as they passed his commentary position, the carriage turned a corner and went out of his sight. Said Henry: 'And now the Queen's gone round the bend!'

But one of the best gaffes of all was perpetrated recently by a lady journalist when writing about our world champion motor cyclist Barry Sheene. She described him as the glamorous sportsman with that throbbing power between his legs! I think that caps anything which we broadcasters have said.

Tenth Over Sadness and joy

It was with much sadness that in September 1976 I heard of the death of Arthur Gilligan at the age of eighty-one. I had seen him at Lord's earlier in the summer, looking and sounding as well as ever, and telling me about his skiing holiday in the winter. For years he and I used to swop stories, and it was my great pleasure when one of mine was rewarded by his cheerful laugh.

Arthur was an old friend of my father-in-law in the twenties and used to stay with him when Sussex were playing Yorkshire. Just after I had married Pauline in 1948 I was looking through her family scrapbook and saw a photograph of Pauline as a very young girl sitting on Arthur's knee. So the next time I saw him I said that I had a bone to pick with him. He looked somewhat perturbed and asked me what it was.

'Arthur,' I said, 'I see that you have been dangling my wife on your knee, and I'd rather you didn't do it again.' He looked so puzzled and upset that I quickly explained to him what I was referring to.

I used to see Arthur play at the Saffrons when I was at my preparatory school at Eastbourne. He was then – in the early twenties – a very fast bowler, magnificent mid-off and a dashing hard-hitting batsman. His 1924–5 side to Australia was probably the most popular to go there this century, though admittedly they did lose and that always helps! But there is no doubt that ever after that he himself was one of the best loved Englishmen in Australia. Not just because of his sporting captaincy but because of his great popularity down under as a cricket commentator. He spoke in a natural, friendly way and even when he could bring himself to criticise, he did it kindly. He formed a famous double act with his old adversary and great friend Vic Richardson. They always backed each other up and never disagreed with what the other said. 'In my opinion he was plumb out. What do you think, Vic?' 'I quite agree Arthur.' Or, 'I'd say the pitch is taking spin now, Arthur.' 'Yes, I quite agree, Vic.'

It may sound trite now but all I can say is that it created a very friendly atmosphere and made pleasant listening. Arthur knew he tended to agree with everyone but told me how on one occasion, it had helped him out of a mess. Once on a hot day during a Headingley Test he fell asleep after lunch and as he dozed he vaguely heard Rex Alston's voice droning on without taking in what he was saying. Suddenly he woke with a start as Rex nudged him in the ribs and said: 'That's how I saw it. What do you say Arthur?'

Arthur reacted quickly for one who had only just woken up. 'I entirely agree with everything you have just said, Rex,' he replied, as his chin sunk once more into his chest. Being Arthur, no one saw anything funny in his reply.

He also swore it was true that a lady once came up to him at a Test and gave him a packet of indigestion tablets. 'Will you please give these to Brian Statham, Mr Gilligan?' 'Yes, of course I will, but why?' replied Arthur. 'Oh,' said the lady, 'I heard you say on the radio that Statham wasn't bowling as fast as usual as he was having trouble with the wind'!

Another friend of mine – and of cricket – who died in the spring of 1977 was Charles Cobham, whom we all knew at Eton as Bargy Lyttelton. He was a big man in every sense of the word, with a tremendous knowledge of cricket – its history, records and playing techniques. He was a superb raconteur and after-dinner speaker with a fund of stories about players past and present, each one accompanied by his own brand of chuckle.

At Eton he never got a cricket colour but played in Middle Club – the equivalent I suppose of the seventh or eighth XI in the school. He bowled prodigious spinners. He made them appear to be more threatening than they were by snapping the fingers of his *left* hand at the exact moment he delivered the ball with his *right*. He could always hit a cricket

October 1975: The first *DYW* on its return from exile. The village is Lacock in Wilts. B.J. and 'victims' are outside the fifteenth century inn, the Angel. (Copyright *Radio Times*)

All at sea aboard cruise ship S.S. *Canberra*. Left to right: Douggie Barnes, engineer, B.J., Commodore Frank Woolley and Anthony Smith, producer.

Well played, sir! B.J. bats at Standish C.C. (Lancs) with chairman Guy Hisley (l.) and vice-president Fred Bazley (r.) in the slips.

B.J. interviews playleader Tricia Barnes at the Jonathan Page adventure playground, Aylesbury. (Copyright *Bucks Herald Aylesbury*)

Say neigh! B.J. chats with Joanna Vardon and friend. (See p. 55)

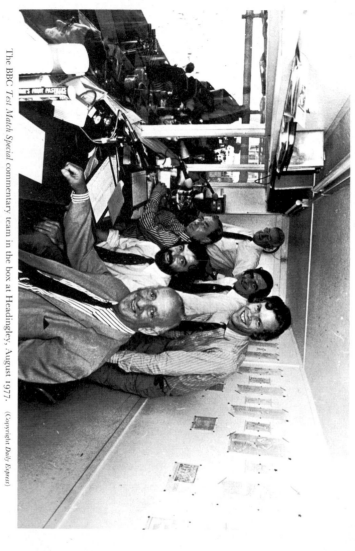

The BBC *Test Match Special* commentary team in the box at Headingley, August 1977. (*Copyright Daily Express*)